THE SOUND OF
STEVE HACKETT

A Selection of Guitar Transcriptions
from His Solo Career

Paulo De Carvalho

ISBN: 0692854347
ISBN-13: 978-0692854341

Cover photographs: © Bill Banasiewicz (top, with electric guitar)
© Lee Millward (bottom, with acoustic guitar)

All other photographs: © Paulo De Carvalho

To my family and friends,
in particular Maluh, Gabriel, Giulia,
Rose, Monique, and Nando,
who have always wanted
to be present in my life.

CONTENTS

FOREWORD

Paulo De Carvalho has put together this unique book which combines transcriptions for a bunch of my pieces with photographs and detailed descriptions of my techniques, featuring instruments and equipment I used to record those tracks.

Paulo takes an electric trip down memory lane which I hope proves helpful to anyone who would like to learn how to play these songs.

February 11, 2017.

PREFACE

Steve Hackett is a prominent musician whose talent surpasses dexterity in performing progressive rock: seeking texture and colors have always been his mark. A self taught professional, he has never allowed himself to be sidetracked by showing-off his technique: for him technique must exist only to exalt musicality. Indeed Steve's sound has caused an enormous impact on my career. I have always spent hours listening to his recordings, writing down notes, playing parts of his songs on my guitar trying to figure out how Steve came up to produce a particular sound or effect. This was the propeller motor for me to write this book.

I decided to get in touch with Steve to propose to transcribe for the guitar some of his solo career songs in order to publish a songbook. The idea of having his songs available to the public as music sheets with chords and tablatures revised by him attracted Steve, especially because guitar players throughout the world would have trustworthy material to play with. We stayed in touch and for about four years we worked together.

A mixing of a book and a songbook, the most relevant and differentiating fact about this work certainly is that, to the moment of its publication, a songbook on Steve's solo career has never been released. While carefully transcribing his music, I had the privilege of, in different moments, asking him questions about fingerings, chord shapes, techniques, timbre, and musical gears that he used. Steve carefully revised the information that I added to the book. Because of that, the present songbook contains authentic transcriptions and it perpetuates in written some of Steve's music.

The songbook recalls events from many years ago and it required hours of conversations with Steve about his versatility both as a guitarist and composer. In this matter, it innovates the concept of songbook, stretching its meaning by providing pioneering guitar transcriptions, all done by me. At the same time it stresses the techniques used by Steve and it evidences the investigation on the instruments, gears and techniques chosen by Steve, which he explained in detail. The result points directly to his unique and distinguished sound – as per the title of the songbook.

Steve Hackett (right) explains details of his techniques to Paulo De Carvalho (left) in his home in London, UK.

The songbook is a product of meticulous research. Besides the discussions with Steve, the sources were based on communications with people that had worked directly for, and with Steve. These included: Jo Hackett, composer, Steve's wife and co-manager; John Hackett, Steve's brother, a flautist, composer and guitarist who has recorded and composed with Steve; Amanda Lehmann, singer and guitarist who sang in many of Steve's live shows and recordings; Pete Cornish, who built pedalboards for Steve throughout his career; and Richard Buckland, guitar tech and production coordinator of Steve's concerts from 1992 to present.

Besides those, other people were with me on this work, among who I would like to mention: Sérgio Lestingi and José Zagury, who provided material that lead me to an accurate listening of the songs in order to write the guitar transcriptions, Maluh De Felice, who edited the text, and Ivo de Carvalho, who helped me with many of the pictures included in the book.

Paulo (left) shows Steve (right) in Fort Lauderdale, US, a preliminary selection of guitar transcriptions.

Choosing what songs would be in the songbook was not an easy task. Few musicians have as vast amount of work to their credit as Steve does, ranging from classical to rock. The valuable collaboration and receptivity of Steve and Jo were of utmost importance to the selection. Steve gave the final approval of the list of songs to be included in the book. Dr. Marcos Nogueira, pianist and composer, professor of Graduate Studies at the School of Music of the Federal University of Rio de Janeiro, reviewed the guitar transcriptions.

Since the beginning I felt the need to provide the reader a chronological sequence of Steve's career, not only for organizational purposes, but mainly because I found out that Steve's varied history led him to build his most unique sound and musical identity, which are the main objects of this songbook.

I came up with three musical eras:

- *Era I: Developing Musicality and Professional Beginning*, which describes the musical environment that Steve lived since an early age, and the acquisition of an harmonica, his first instrument. With the harmonica Steve recorded his first track, which was with the band *Canterbury Glass*. This section ends reporting Steve's first entire album, *The Road*, recorded with the band *Quiet World*.

- *Era II: Finding His Sound* starts with the *Genesis Era* moving on to expose many of the techniques, guitars and pedalboards used by Steve.

- *Era III: Steve's Solo Career* provides a selection of guitar transcriptions from Steve's Solo Career, all written by me.

In each of Steve's musical eras I proposed, Steve was developing different approaches, and creating new techniques, as evidenced throughout the book.

Upon thorough investigation, I came up with charts that showcased Steve's instruments and gears in each musical era. I was careful to make visible and clear the connections Steve chose to better produce the sound that he was searching for in each album, live and/or in studio. In this matter, Pete Cornish's contribution makes public, for the first time, information on a signal path on two of Steve's pedalboards. Steve has revised all these charts that are, therefore, very reliable.

Aside from the two pictures of the cover by Bill Banasiewicz (top) and Lee Millward (bottom), the book includes unpublished photographs of Steve's hands on the guitar showing details of his techniques. I took these pictures at Steve's live performances as well as in his home. You will also find numerous unpublished photos of Steve's original instruments and pedalboards, all taken by me.

In accordance with its title, this songbook is not just about music sheets, charts and tablatures. It is about the music that has shaped the legendary Steve Hackett. Above all, it is about Steve's sound.

Hope you enjoy it!

Paulo De Carvalho

In Miami, US, Paulo (left) shows Steve (right) details subsequently added to the guitar transcriptions.

ERA I - DEVELOPING MUSICALITY AND PROFESSIONAL BEGINNING

Steve comes from a family that deeply appreciates music. His father used to play a number of instruments, including: the clarinet, the guitar and the harmonica. Born on February 12th, 1950, Steve, at age two, already had his own harmonica. When he was four years old, Steve had performed solos on it and at age six he got a more sophisticated harmonica: a chromatic one. In 1962, at age twelve, Steve began to compose on his own. In the same year, his father brought him, from Canada, a Kay f-hole, a steel-string guitar that was big for Steve and that had a very large range. Even though it was challenging to play, Steve immediately fell in love with its vibrant sounds.

The youngster's interest in classical music started by chance, during a visit with a friend who was sick, and played a recording of Tchaikovsky's Piano Concerto in B Flat Minor for him. Later on, he became impassioned with the music of Johann Sebastian Bach when he heard Segovia playing its Gavotte BWV 1012 arranged for the guitar from the original Cello Suite #6 in D Major. He was intrigued, for many years, by the idea that someone could play that piece on the guitar. Indeed, in 2008 he, himself, recorded that same piece on the album *Tribute*.

The electric guitar was becoming more and more of a priority in Steve's attentiveness to music. He was getting very impressed with King Crimson - one of his first influences, in addition to: The Shadows, The Beatles, The Rolling Stones, Muddy Waters, and Sonny Terry. In 1966 he dropped out of school to work in different jobs while placing advertisements in *Melody Maker,* a British weekly pop/rock music magazine, searching for musicians to form a band to play in local gigs.

In 1968 Steve recorded his first track in which he basically played the harmonica. The album was *Sacred Scenes and Characters* with the band *Canterbury Glass*. In the next year he became part of the group *Quiet World*, which did not play live shows, but with whom he recorded his first entire album *The Road*. Around this time Steve bought a Gibson Melody Maker, whose sound resembled the one of a Les Paul, a more expensive model that attracted him. It was primarily because many great musicians such as Eric Clapton, Peter Green and Robert Fripp were using it. He already had a twelve-string Yamaha guitar, a Colorsound Wha+Fuzz pedal and an Ampeg amplifier.

Gears : Quiet World (1969-1970)

1 - Gibson Melody Maker
2 - Yamaha 12 strings Gtr
3 - Harmonica
4 - Colorsound Wha+Fuzz
5 - Volume Pedal
6 - Ampeg Amp

ERA II - FINDING HIS SOUND

Genesis Era

In 1970 Steve decided to change the advertisement he was placing for five years in the British weekly pop/rock newspaper *Melody Maker*. He wanted to play in a band in which he could also play in live shows. In other to make it more attractive, Steve had the idea to write a more pretentious advertisement: "Imaginative guitarist/writer seeks involvement with receptive musicians, determined to strive beyond existing stagnant music forms".

At that time, Anthony Phillips, one of the founders of the group *Genesis*, had just left the band, and *Genesis* was looking for a guitarist. Peter Gabriel called Steve and they agreed that Tony Banks and Peter Gabriel were to meet Steve at his flat. Steve however was asked to first listen to the album *Trespass* by Genesis, especially the song *Stagnation*. Steve played for Tony Banks and Peter Gabriel. The performance consisted of three songs with different styles. In the first song, Steve used a twelve-string guitar and he was accompanied by his brother John on the flute. Five years later, this selection became part of one of Steve's songs, *The Hermit* in his first album solo *Voyage of the Acolyte*. Steve used an electric guitar to showcase his second song, an atonal music - a mix of Hendrix and Stravinsky. The harmonica was the instrument chosen by Steve for the third song, but Peter Gabriel mentioned that its sound did not match *Genesis* style. Indeed, Steve never used the harmonica while playing with *Genesis*.

Gears : Nursery Cryme (Live Jan 1971- Aug 1972) (Studio Aug 1971)

1 - Gibson Les Paul Custom
2 - Gibson Melody Maker
3 - Hagstrom BJ-12
4 - Marshall Supa Fuzz
5 - Shaftesbury Duo Fuzz
6 - Schaller Volume Pedal
7 - Hiwatt 100w Head
8 - Hiwatt 150w 4x12 Cabinets

After some gigs with guitarist Mick Barnard, *Genesis* officially began with Steve Hackett on the guitar, having its first concert with the new formation on January, 14th, 1971. As Steve started with *Genesis*, he requested a Les Paul and a Hiwatt amplifier, but in the beginning he also played with a *Gibson Melody Maker*. During this time with Genesis, Steve used a Marshall Supa Fuzz, a Fuzz Shafesbury duo and a Schaller pedal volume. He worked hard to create a new sound color on the guitar that would characterize Genesis' tone style.

Nursery Cryme, Steve's first album with *Genesis,* already had Steve's trademark sound which included the use of volume swell and tapping*. Steve used the Hiwatt amplifier. This was Steve Hackett's real first album: if in the previous albums he was only playing, in this one Steve had a great role in the composition, arrangements and styles.

*Please refer to *Steve's Techniques* on pages 18 and 19.

Another of Steve's feature from the Genesis Era was that he sometimes used the Fuzz pedal with a saturated Fuzz tone. He used the guitar with a neck pickup which had its tone control all the way back, removing the high frequencies, and helping to diminish the noise created by the Fuzz.

On the track *Music Box* Steve used Varyspeed and Tonebender.

Foxtrot album was all recorded with a *Fender Champ* amp, except on the track *Horizons*, one of the most famous classical songs ever written for the guitar, in which he used a steel-string Yamaha guitar plugged into a *Leslie* - a combined amplifier with a two-way loudspeaker usually associated with Hammond organ.

At this time Steve began to use the Wah-wah pedal

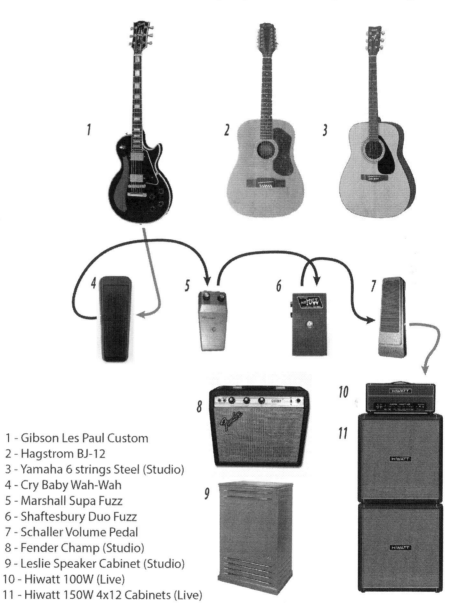

Gears : Foxtrot (Studio Aug, Sep1972) (Live Sep 1972 to Aug 1973)

1 - Gibson Les Paul Custom
2 - Hagstrom BJ-12
3 - Yamaha 6 strings Steel (Studio)
4 - Cry Baby Wah-Wah
5 - Marshall Supa Fuzz
6 - Shaftesbury Duo Fuzz
7 - Schaller Volume Pedal
8 - Fender Champ (Studio)
9 - Leslie Speaker Cabinet (Studio)
10 - Hiwatt 100W (Live)
11 - Hiwatt 150W 4x12 Cabinets (Live)

before the Fuzz in order to add different tone quality, giving a boost in certain frequencies in a single position. He used fuzz with a two-way switch to create high harmonics.

Genesis Live, a recording of the shows of the *Foxtrot* tour, is the group's first live album.

After that came *Selling England by the Pound*, considered by Hackett the best Genesis' album ever. One of its greatest moment was the solo of *Firth of Fifth*, in which Steve used Colorsound Fuzz box, Echoplex, Schiller volume pedal, and a Hi-Watt amp. In the song *Dancing with the Moonlit Knight*, Steve used Tonebender and Duo Fuzz. Colorsound Octivider pedal was used both in *Dancing with the Moonlit Knight* and *Battle of Epping Forest*, as well as in *Colony of Slippermen* in Genesis' following album *Lamb Lies Down on Broadway*.

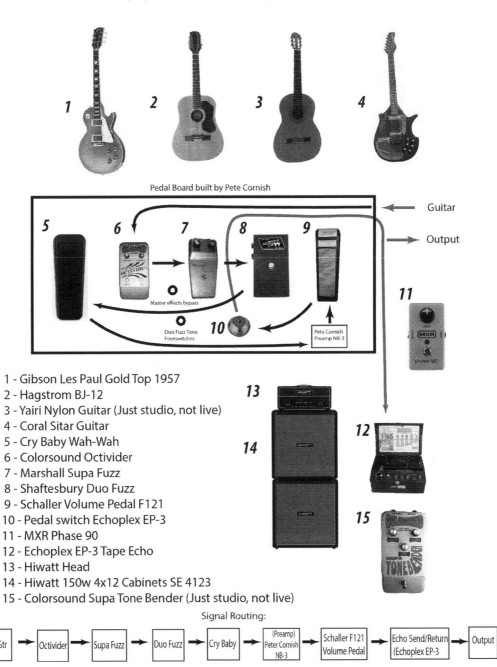

Gears : Selling England by The Pound (Studio Aug 1973) (Live Sep 1973 - May 1974)

Pedal Board built by Pete Cornish

Guitar

Output

Master effects bypass

Duo Fuzz Tone Footswitches

Pete Cornish Preamp NB-3

1 - Gibson Les Paul Gold Top 1957
2 - Hagstrom BJ-12
3 - Yairi Nylon Guitar (Just studio, not live)
4 - Coral Sitar Guitar
5 - Cry Baby Wah-Wah
6 - Colorsound Octivider
7 - Marshall Supa Fuzz
8 - Shaftesbury Duo Fuzz
9 - Schaller Volume Pedal F121
10 - Pedal switch Echoplex EP-3
11 - MXR Phase 90
12 - Echoplex EP-3 Tape Echo
13 - Hiwatt Head
14 - Hiwatt 150w 4x12 Cabinets SE 4123
15 - Colorsound Supa Tone Bender (Just studio, not live)

Signal Routing:

Gtr → Octivider → Supa Fuzz → Duo Fuzz → Cry Baby → (Preamp) Peter Cornish NB-3 → Schaller F121 Volume Pedal → Echo Send/Return (Echoplex EP-3 → Output

For the album *The Lamb Lies Down on Broadway* Steve composed splendid songs, such as *Cuckoo Cocoon*. In the song that has the same name as the album, Steve used terrific effects such as the ones using two fuzzes simulating a fly buzzing.

Gears : The Lamb Lies Down on Broadway (Studio Aug-Oct 1974) (Live Nov 1974 - May 1975)

1 - Gibson Les Paul Gold Top 1957
2 - Yairi Nylon (1973) (Studio)
3 - Zemaitis Custom 12 strings (Studio)
4- Coral Sitar Guitar (Studio)
5 - Cry Baby Wah-Wah
6 - Colorsound Octivider
7 - Marshall Supa Fuzz
8 - Shaftesbury Duo Fuzz
9 - Schaller Volume Pedal F121
10 -Pedal Switch for Echoplex EP-3
11 - MXR Phase 90
12 - Echoplex EP-3 Tape Echo
13 - EMS Synthi Hi-Fli
14- Shure SM57 (Studio)
15 - Leslie (Studio)
16 - Fender Champ (Studio)
17 - HH 100W IC100 (Live)
18 - Hiwatt 150w 4x12 Cabinets SE4123 (Live)

(EMT-140 plate reverb mixdown)

Signal Routing:

Gtr1 → Octivider → Supa Fuzz → Duo Fuzz → Cry Baby → (Preamp) Peter Cornish NB-3 → Schaller F121 Volume Pedal → Echo Send/Return (Echoplex EP-3 → Output

After the end of *The Lamb* tour, Peter Gabriel left the band and Steve recorded his first album solo *Voyage of the Acolyte*, followed by two *Genesis* studio albums: *A Trick of the Tail* and *Wind & Wuthering* - and one *Genesis* live album: *Seconds Out*, which was part of the *Wind & Wuthering* tour.

A Trick of the Tail included some of Steve's well-known songs such as *Entangled, Dance on a Volcano, Los Endos*, and *Ripples*. In the later Steve used a EMS Synthi Hi-Fli to add more texture, and he performed an amazing solo which had a mysterious mood. Steve had previously used this effect on the solo of the track *Counting Out Time* in *The Lamb Lies Down on Broadway*.

Wind & Wuthering contained songs using classical guitar, with *Blood on the Rooftops* being one of them.

After *Wind & Wuthering*, the live album *Second Out* was released, having been acclaimed one of the best live albums of all times. Along with the guitar in live concerts, Steve played the Taurus Pedal Bass taking turns with Mike Rutherford on the songs *Squonk, Los Endos* and *Supper's Ready*.

During the mixing phase of *Second Out*, Steve left Genesis to invest time on his solo career. By then, Steve had spent seven years with *Genesis*.

Genesis had an enormous influence on Steve's career, just like Steve had had an enormous influence on *Genesis*. During the Genesis Era, Steve had the chance to experiment with different structures and forms of songs at the same time that he had to act like an orchestral player, blending sound elements with other musicians in order to put together a compelling performance.

Gear- A Trick of the Tail (Studio Oct - Nov 1975) (Live Mar - Jul 1976)
Gear- Wind & Wuthering (Studio Sep - Oct 1976) (Live Jan - Jul 1977)

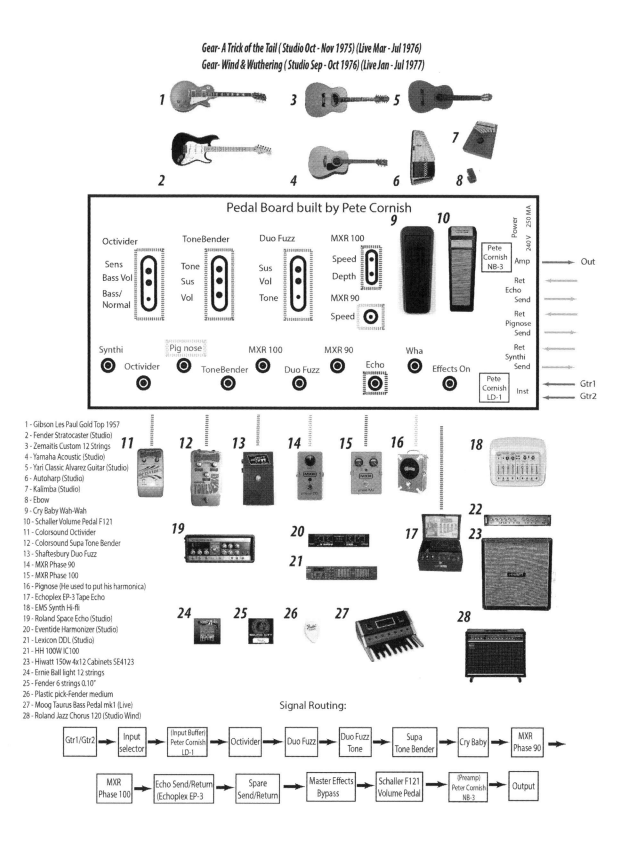

1 - Gibson Les Paul Gold Top 1957
2 - Fender Stratocaster (Studio)
3 - Zemaitis Custom 12 Strings
4 - Yamaha Acoustic (Studio)
5 - Yari Classic Alvarez Guitar (Studio)
6 - Autoharp (Studio)
7 - Kalimba (Studio)
8 - Ebow
9 - Cry Baby Wah-Wah
10 - Schaller Volume Pedal F121
11 - Colorsound Octivider
12 - Colorsound Supa Tone Bender
13 - Shaftesbury Duo Fuzz
14 - MXR Phase 90
15 - MXR Phase 100
16 - Pignose (He used to put his harmonica)
17 - Echoplex EP-3 Tape Echo
18 - EMS Synth Hi-fli
19 - Roland Space Echo (Studio)
20 - Eventide Harmonizer (Studio)
21 - Lexicon DDL (Studio)
21 - HH 100W IC100
23 - Hiwatt 150w 4x12 Cabinets SE4123
24 - Ernie Ball light 12 strings
25 - Fender 6 strings 0.10"
26 - Plastic pick-Fender medium
27 - Moog Taurus Bass Pedal mk1 (Live)
28 - Roland Jazz Chorus 120 (Studio Wind)

Signal Routing:

Gtr1/Gtr2 → Input selector → (Input Buffer) Peter Cornish LD-1 → Octivider → Duo Fuzz → Duo Fuzz Tone → Supa Tone Bender → Cry Baby → MXR Phase 90 →

MXR Phase 100 → Echo Send/Return (Echoplex EP-3 → Spare Send/Return → Master Effects Bypass → Schaller F121 Volume Pedal → (Preamp) Peter Cornish NB-3 → Output

Steve's Techniques

Steve is a self taught guitarist who has picked up techniques from watching other people, besides creating his own. He has never seen the guitar as a musical instrument itself, but rather as a tool to reproduce different colors and sounds. One example of that is when he simulates the violin using the volume pedal.

In terms of musicality, Steve guides himself more by feelings than by theories. Not only has Steve Hackett shaped the music, but the music has shaped Steve Hackett.

An accident on his left wrist, meeting up with a broken piece of glass before the beginning of Genesis' *The Lamb Lies Down on Broadway* tour, forced Steve to adapt his unique way of playing, resulting in a restructure of his techniques. The following are some of these techniques.

VIBRATO

Tone quality is the most meaningful musical identity for Steve Hackett. In his opinion, one single note played with perfect tone is more important than a hundred virtuoso fast notes played without attention. Because of that, the technique that he has devoted more time in his career to is the vibrato. Although he has always had an admirable vibrato, he believes that he was only able to do it the proper way around the year 2000.

For years he practiced it very carefully and he realized that he had to bend up the string with three fingers (photo 1) and then bend down and up repeatedly very slowly and very widely, speeding it up little by little.

One can play free standing vibrato, without the support of the thumb (photo 2), which is less controllable and more risky, but which allows the musician to successfully perform a faster vibrato. Vibrato must end in upright position so that it does not sound flat (photo 3).

  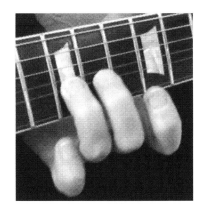

photo 1: Steve bending up the string using three fingers, in order to have a nice vibrato

photo 2: Steve playing free standing vibrato, without the support of the thumb, for faster vibrato

photo 3: Steve showing upright position - end position of the vibrato- in order to not sound flat

LEGATO

Legato is a smooth, flowing manner of playing. In order to produce a legato sound, Steve's plays with less picking, using hammer-on and pull-off, and sometimes just sliding.

Example: the excerpt from *Love Song to a Vampire* from Steve's solo album *Wolflight*.

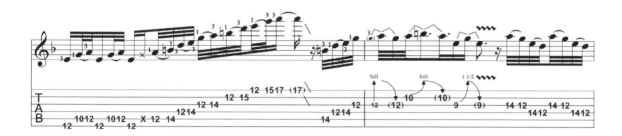

SLIDE RING

The guitar ring is a stainless steel ring placed on the right pinky. It gives great mobility to produce a sliding effect on the string and it can stay on the performer's hand during most of the performance (photo 4).

photo 4: Steve using slide ring in concert.
Fort Lauderdale, US, April 14ᵗʰ, 2016

SWEEP PICKING

Sweep Picking is a technique that Steve used in the song *Dancing with the Moonlit Knight* on Genesis' album *Selling England by the Pound* (1973).

The technique consists of playing single notes on consecutive strings, one at a time, with a "sweeping" motion of the pick: picking across the strings and then back again, doing it very fast, copying the chord strokes of bowed string instruments.

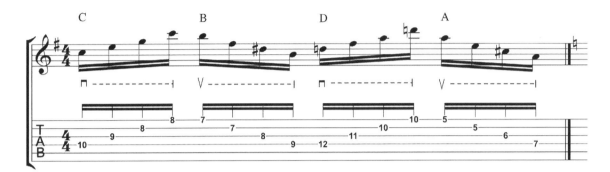

TREMOLO ARM

Steve uses the tremolo arm in two ways to produce different sounds: in the first way, he taps the tremolo arm repeatedly with the palm of the right hand in a fast way (photos 5, 6, 7); in the second way, he pulls hard the tremolo arm many times letting it go each time (photos 8, 9, 10). Steve likes to call this last effect *bubble*.

Tremolo Arm, 1ˢᵗ way: Steve tapping the tremolo arm

photo 5   photo 6   photo 7

Tremolo Arm, 2ⁿᵈ way (bubble): Steve pulling hard on the tremolo arm

photo 8   photo 9   photo 10

*Photos taken on April 14ᵗʰ, 2016 at Steve's concert in Fort Lauderdale, US.

FLAMENCO AND CLASSICAL

Among other techniques in nylon string guitar, Steve uses *flamenco guitar style* and *classical fingerstyle*. It is important to practice these techniques very slowly because they must sound clean and fluent in order to sound legato. In addition, guitar players must let the strings ring throughout, and they should phrase and practice with dynamics.

Flamenco Guitar Style

Example: intro of the *Love Song to a Vampire* from the album *Wolflight*.

Flamenco Rasqueado

One type of *flamenco rasqueado* technique is the one in which the guitar player starts strumming an upstroke, one finger at a time, playing respectively the pinky (photo 11), the annular (photo 12), the middle (photo 13) and the index (photo 14) fingers. It is a percussive strumming.

Steve showing a flamenco rasqueado with an upstroke

photo 11: Steve starts the flamenco rasqueado with the pinky

photo 12: then Steve plays with the annular

photo 13: after that, Steve uses the middle finger

photo 14: Steve finishes the flamenco rasqueado with the index finger

Love Song to a Vampire is an example of a song where Steve uses *flamenco rasqueado**.

* Please refer to page 122, measure 24.

Classical Fingerstyle

Example: the excerpt of the introduction of the track *Horizons*
from the album *Genesis Revisited: Live at The Royal Albert Hall*:

Moderate ♩ = *112*

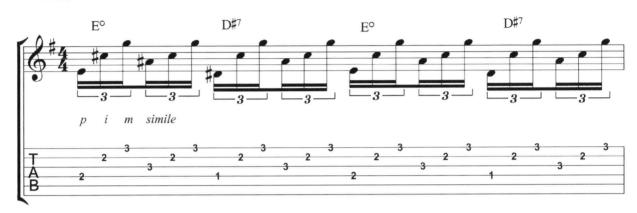

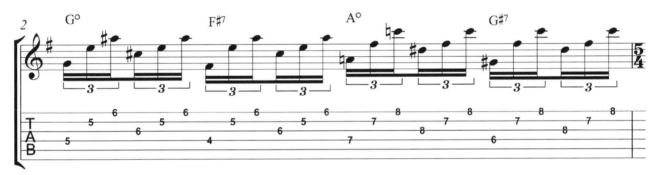

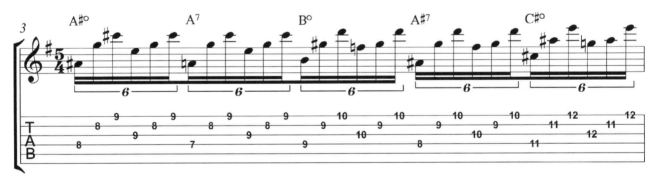

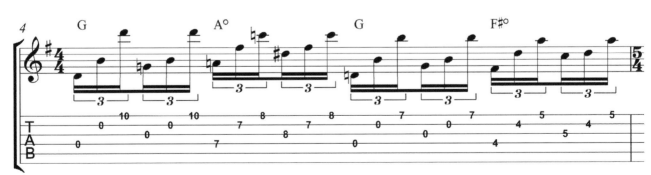

2

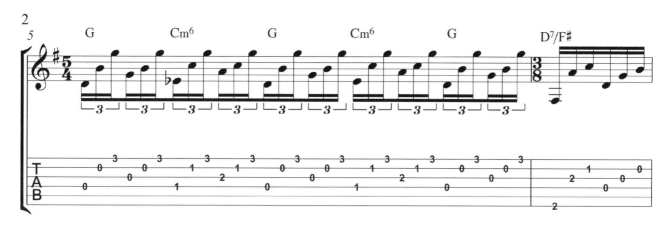

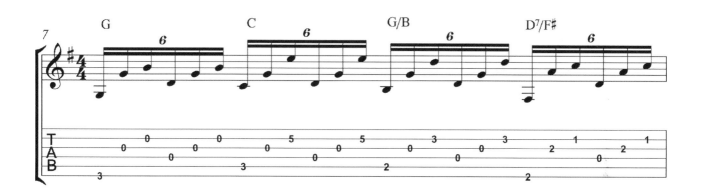

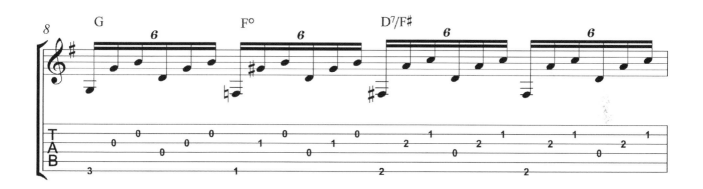

SUSTAINED NOTE

Steve has always been a master in sustaining long notes. In his early professional years, he used to play sitting close to the amp in order to position the guitar next to it whenever he needed to extend a note in feedback. According to Steve, that worked in nine out of ten times. A few years later, in 1976/77, he began to use EBow to produce the same long note. Nowadays he uses a Fernandes guitar with sustained pickup to produce the same effect. From Steve's experience, the later worked 99 % of the time, being a more trustful choice.

The solo of *Firth of Fifth* from the album *Selling England by the Pound*, considered by many one of the best solos ever recorded, is one of Steve's masterpieces in sustained notes. Steve used a Gibson LesPaul Golden Top, with Coloursound Fuzz box, Echoplex and Schiller volume pedal and Hi-Watt amp. Below is an excerpt of this solo:

VOLUME SWELL

Besides its normal use, Steve uses the volume pedal to make the guitar sound like a violin. This is called *volume swell*.

To obtain this effect the guitar player must attack the string with the volume off and subsequently turn it up to produce a crescendo. The contact of the pick with the string should not be heard.

Most of the time Steve uses the volume pedal after the Fuzzes, but since *Nursery Cryme*, the first album he recorded with *Genesis*, Steve has also used the volume pedal before the Fuzzes, as in the songs *The Fountain of Salmacis* and *Seven Stones* on the same album.

TAPPING

Usually the name of a technique appears years after it has been played. In 1971 when Steve played the solo on the track *Musical Box*, in the album *Nursery Cryme*, he named a specific sound effect *nailing*. The same effect was later called *tapping* by Van Halen, and since then it is noted by the later.

Steve likes to use tapping as a tone effect, as when he marries the guitar with the keyboard - so that the mix of the sound of the two instruments sounds like a new, barely known timbre.

In this technique, Steve bends the index finger in a way that its entire nail touches the string (photo 15), but sometimes he can also use the pad of the tip of the index finger (photo 16). If the note is below the 12th fret, Steve usually uses the bent index with the entire nail touching the string. If the note is on the 12th fret or above it, Steve usually uses the pad of the tip of the index.

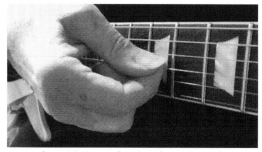
photo 15: Steve showing the entire nail touching the string

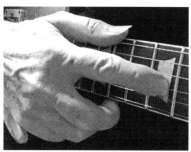
photo 16: Steve using the pad of the tip of the index finger

Tapping requires maximum ability with minimum movement as in the bridge of the song *Shadow of the Hierophant* from the album *Voyage of the Acolyte* (1975):

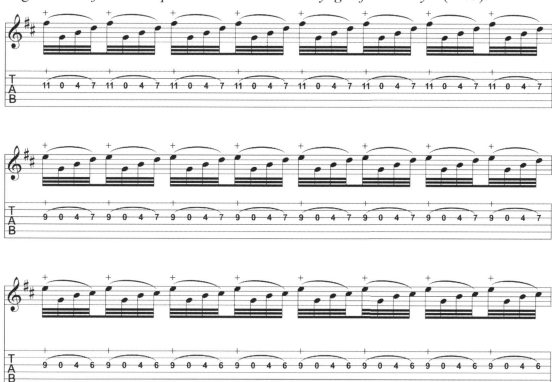

NAIL PICK

Steve used to play with the pick during the Genesis Era. Nowadays Steve mostly uses his nail. He rarely uses the plectrum. He saves it for when he has to strum the strings really hard.

The way Steve uses the nail as a pick includes, in many times, the use of the pad of the index finger in the upstroke. This is a different way of playing classical guitar, in which the nail is mostly used.

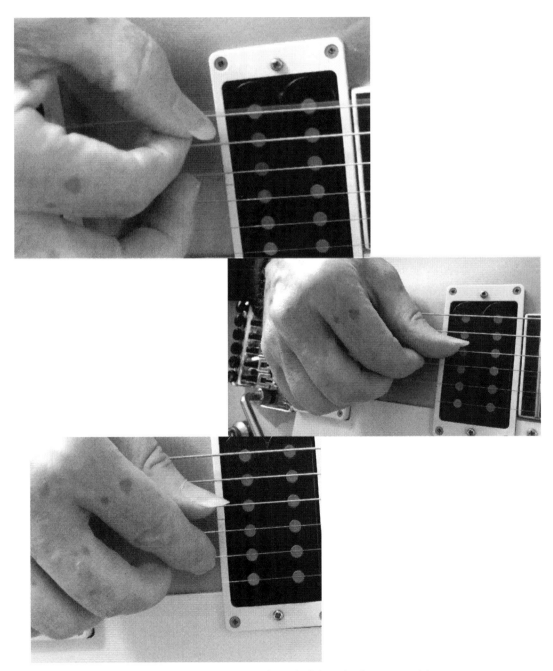

photos 17 - 19: Steve using the pad of the index finger as a pick

Steve's Guitars

Gibson Guitar

Steve bought a Les Paul Goldtop 1957 - which is one of his trademarks - in New York, in December 1972, while playing on the first Genesis US tour. It is made of mahogany with maple cap, with Tune-o-matic bridge and PAF humbuckers.

The first album he recorded with this guitar was *Selling England by The Pound* (1973).

Before the Les Paul Goldtop 1957 Steve had several Gibsons: one Melody Maker, some Black Les Paul Customs, and a Les Paul Sunburst.

Photos 20 - 24: Steve's Les Paul Gold Top 1957

Fernandes Guitar

The Japanese company *Fernandes* built Steve a customized guitar which resembled his Les Paul Goldtop 1957. Aside from the tone quality, the main differences between the two guitars are that, besides having a tremolo arm, the Fernandes has a sustainer pickup, which allows the performer to get a sustained sound without having a high volume in the amp. In addition, the Fernandes allows the guitarist to easily get an upper-harmonic.

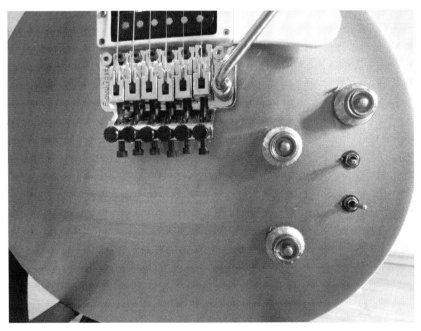

Photos 25 – 27: Steve's Fernandes Guitar

Steve's Pedalboards by Pete Cornish

Pete Cornish is one of the most acknowledged people in the rock industry, who has built pedalboards for Genesis, Queen, Pink Floyd, King Crimson, and The Police, among others. The first system he built for Steve Hackett was ordered by his tech, David Jacobson, and delivered on August 13th, 1973. Its signal routing order was: GTR>Colorsound Octivider>Marshall Supa Fuzz>Shaftesbury Duo Fuzz>Cry Baby>Pete Cornish Preamp (NB-3 preset to +10dB)>Schaller F121 Volume pedal>Echo Send/Return>Single output to amp.

The size of the pedalboard was 44 x 18 inches and it was the first totally mains powered system featuring stabilized +9vdc and also stabilized -9vdc supplies for the effects.There were three extra footswitches: Master effects bypass, Echo S/R bypass and Duo Fuzz Tone. Each pedal on it had its own bypass footswitch and there was no LED or any other light indicator for the effects - just a mains "power on" neon indicator. The *AC Power in* was on a *Bulgin 3* pin plug as used on HiWatt Amps. The input voltage was fixed at 240 vac.

Interesting to note is that when Steve received the pedalboard, his roadie painted it all in black in order for it not to be seen by the audience during the concerts.

By July 1975, Pete Cornish had changed all his designs. By removing the effects from its original cases and placing them inside the pedalboard, just the effect's controls were visible from its top. By doing this, the separation of the footswitches became necessary, but it made possible to add indicator lights for each switch/effect. The lights were filament bulbs in 1/4 inch sealed metal holders and at that time they were only available in red. This was before LEDs were on the market.

One other Pete Cornish's unique innovation was the addition of the now famous *Doughnut* around each footswitch. This protected the switch from sideways forces and it massively increased the system's life expectancy, an idea that until this day he still includes in every stage system that he builds.

Photo 28: Peter Cornish (right) shows Paulo De Carvalho the signal path of Steve's pedalboards in his office in Southern England

Pete Cornish's later system (1976/7*) for Steve consisted of GTR1/GTR2>Input selector> Input Buffer (Pete Cornish LD-1)>Octivider>Duo Fuzz>Duo Fuzz Tone>Tone Bender>Cry Baby>MXR 90>MXR100>Echo Send/Return>Spare Send/ Return >Master Effects Bypass>Schaller F121 Volume Pedal>Pete Cornish Preamp (NB-3 type with preset gain)> Single Output to Amp. There are no pedal boxes on the top of the pedalboard and all of its controls have been added in recessed panels with the same control knobs used throughout. Steve used this system for many years.

* DATE OF REQUEST AND DELIVERY UNKNOWN ACCORDINGLY TO PETE CORNISH.

ERA III - SOLO CAREER

Photos 29 – 32: Steve Hackett in concert.
Fort Lauderdale, US, April 14th, 2016

VOYAGE OF THE ACOLYTE

Steve Hackett's first solo album *Voyage of the Acolyte* was recorded at Kingsway Recorders in London, in the months of June and July, 1975, between the *Lamb* tour and the recording of the album *A Trick of the Tail*. It was released in October, 1975.

Around that time, Steve was fascinated by Tarot cards. Having the image of each card as inspiration resulted in his creating a related theme for each song of the album.

The album had the participation of extraordinary musicians including his bandmates at the time, Phil Collins and Mike Rutherford, his brother John Hackett, as well as John Acock and Sally Oldfield.

HANDS OF THE PRIESTESS, PART 1

Hands of the Priestess, Part 1 represents a reference point for Steve. It was the first song recorded by Steve on his early solo album. Its recording, which included his brother John on the flute, came along with an impressive quality, what gave Steve much confidence.

Genesis' future was uncertain as Peter Gabriel had just left the group, one more reason for Steve to increase the efforts to make it an appealing album.

Hackett created tension in the beginning of this song by playing the C#m(add9)/G# chord, which is: open 1st string E; D# on the 2nd string, 4th fret; C# on the 3rd string, 6th fret; and G# on the 4th string, 6th fret. When he played the note A on the bass, the chord is AMaj7(#4), which is actually the same previous chord C#m(add9)/G# using the note A instead of G# on the bass. Then he played the E chord on the 7th fret, and he kept moving the hand with the same shape by a 1/2 step four times, back and forth to the Am/E chord, making the progression I - IVm. After that came a mysterious Am6/9 with the bass on B, making the progression Em   Em(Maj7)   Fmaj7/A   Eb   C   Adim - then the song went back to E major.

THE LOVERS

The Lovers was a short song with elements that resembled the ones on its following track *Shadow of the Hierophant*. Steve took a piece of the recording of a previous track, *The Hermit*, ran it backwards, and he included it in the midst of *The Lovers*.

Steve began with D9, which is: open 1st string E; F# on the 2nd string, 7th fret; C on the 3rd string, 5th fret. By changing just one note, F# to G, D9 turns into a D9(sus4) chord. Then he went back to D9.

Following that, there were: Em/A   Am   C6/9   C/E   D   C6/9   C/E, moving on to the reversed section.

I took the second part of the music in the way it is heard in the recording, and I transcribed it backwards so that guitar players get to know the song as it was originally composed.

Studio Gears : Voyage of the Acolyte (June - July 1975)

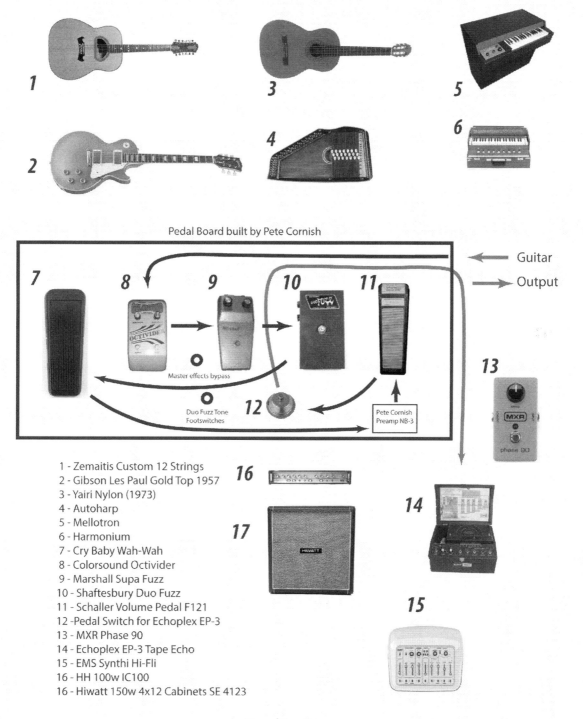

Pedal Board built by Pete Cornish

Guitar
Output

Master effects bypass

Duo Fuzz Tone
Footswitches

Pete Cornish
Preamp NB-3

1 - Zemaitis Custom 12 Strings
2 - Gibson Les Paul Gold Top 1957
3 - Yairi Nylon (1973)
4 - Autoharp
5 - Mellotron
6 - Harmonium
7 - Cry Baby Wah-Wah
8 - Colorsound Octivider
9 - Marshall Supa Fuzz
10 - Shaftesbury Duo Fuzz
11 - Schaller Volume Pedal F121
12 -Pedal Switch for Echoplex EP-3
13 - MXR Phase 90
14 - Echoplex EP-3 Tape Echo
15 - EMS Synthi Hi-Fli
16 - HH 100w IC100
16 - Hiwatt 150w 4x12 Cabinets SE 4123

Signal Routing:

Gtr1 → Octivider → Supa Fuzz → Duo Fuzz → Cry Baby → (Preamp) Peter Cornish NB-3 → Schaller F121 Volume Pedal → Echo Send/Return (Echoplex EP-3) → Output

from Steve Hackett - *Voyage of the Acolyte*

Hands of Priestess Part1

by Steve Hackett

Transcribed by Paulo De Carvalho

♩ = 92

Gtr. 1 (12 string)

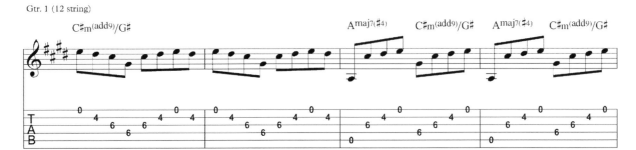

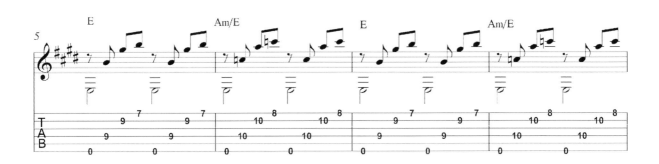

Gtr. 2★ (Flute arr. for gtr)

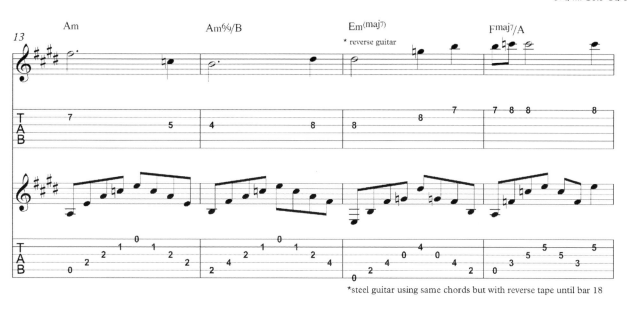

*steel guitar using same chords but with reverse tape until bar 18

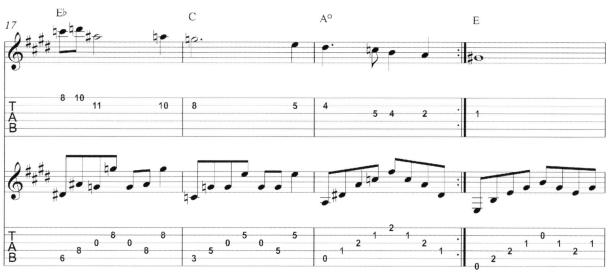

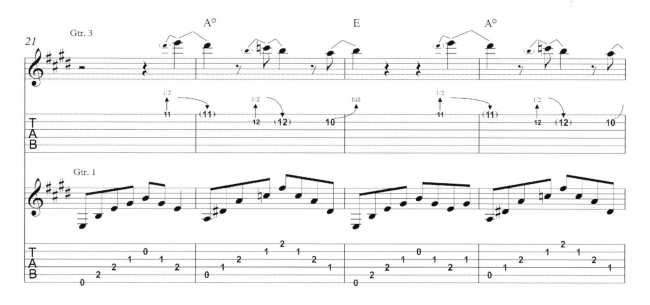

from Steve Hackett - *Voyage of the Acolyte*

The Lovers

by Steve Hackett

Transcribed by Paulo De Carvalho

♩ = 94

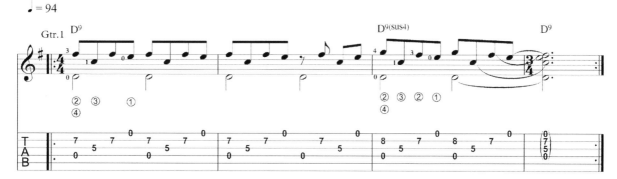

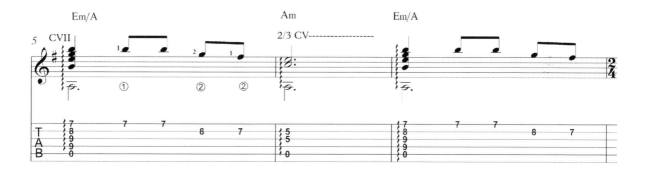

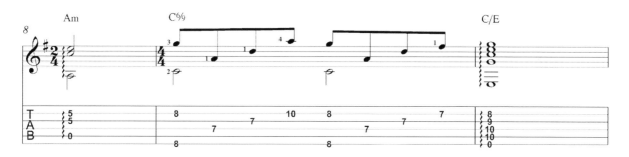

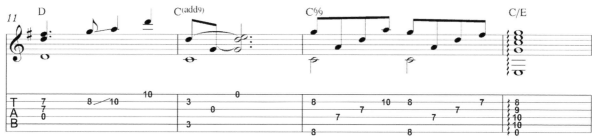

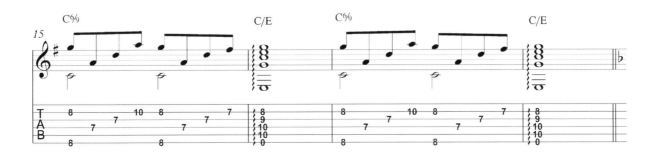

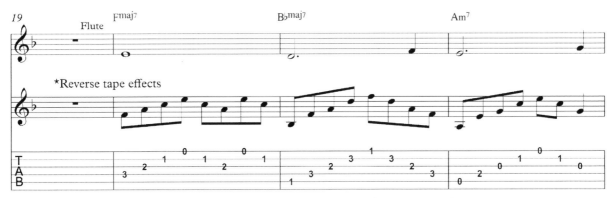

* This is the original take that was used as reverse tape effect (from the Hermit song)

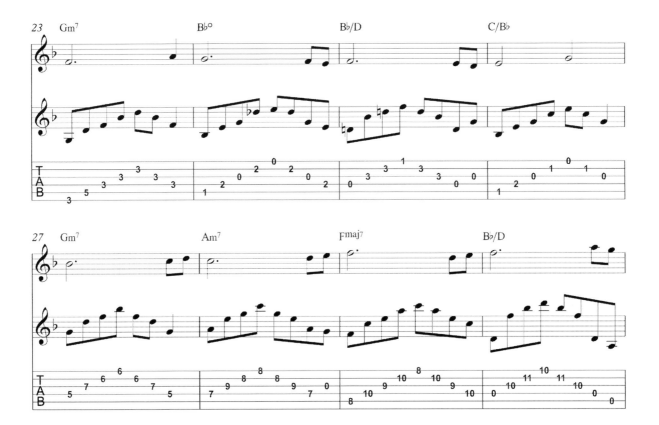

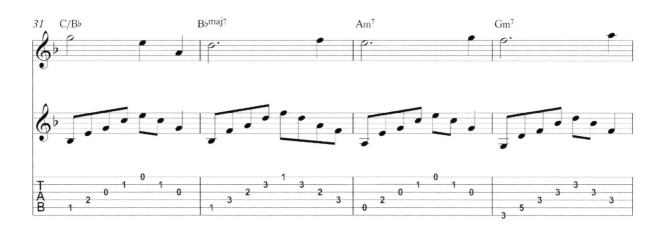

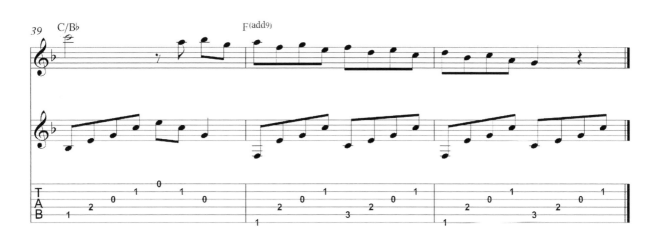

PLEASE DON'T TOUCH

This album was recorded at Cherokee Studios, De Lane Lea Studios, Kingsway, and Record Plant between the months of November 1977 and February 1978. It was released in May 1978.

It was the first solo album after Steve left Genesis and some of its material was written while he was still a member of the group. For its recording he invited a myriad of renowned musicians, including Steve Walsh from *Kansas* and Richie Havens.

HOW CAN I?

An imaginary day in someone's life - his/her relationships and diverse activities - was Steve's inspiration for the song *How can I?*

Steve invited Richie Havens who, in a profound, meaningful way, brought light to the music with his voice. He recorded it on a twelve-string guitar while Richie sang and played percussion simultaneously. Steve also used a Guitar Synthesizer Roland GR 500 reproducing a keyboard sound.

It is relevant to notice that Steve used different shapes for the first three chords of the intro: Cadd2add4, Cadd4 and C, which also happened when Havens began to sing.

On bar 14 Steve used G/F with G on 1st string, 3rd fret; open 2nd, 3rd, and 4th strings, and bass on F on the 6th string, 1st fret. On bar 27, before going back to the beginning of the melody, Steve played D7 instead of Dm as to move into the Dominant G, but instead he went to IV (F/C), going to V (G/F), and then back to C afterwards.

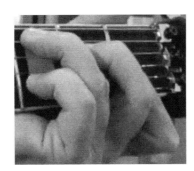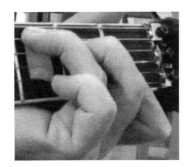

photos 33 - 35: Steve showing, respectively, the different shapes
of the first three chords Cadd2add4 , Cadd4 and C in How Can I?

Studio Gears : Please Don't Touch (Nov 1977-Feb 1978)

Pedal Board built by Pete Cornish

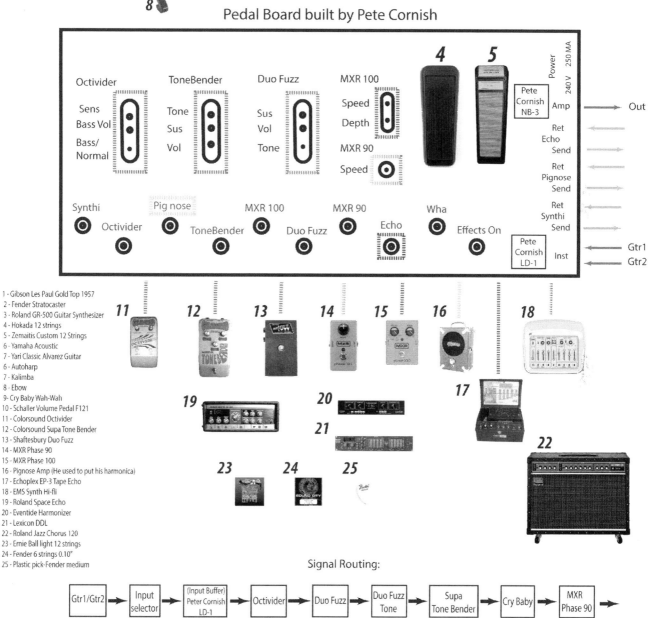

1 - Gibson Les Paul Gold Top 1957
2 - Fender Stratocaster
3 - Roland GR-500 Guitar Synthesizer
4 - Hokada 12 strings
5 - Zemaitis Custom 12 Strings
6 - Yamaha Acoustic
7 - Yari Classic Alvarez Guitar
6 - Autoharp
7 - Kalimba
8 - Ebow
9- Cry Baby Wah-Wah
10 - Schaller Volume Pedal F121
11 - Colorsound Octivider
12 - Colorsound Supa Tone Bender
13 - Shaftesbury Duo Fuzz
14 - MXR Phase 90
15 - MXR Phase 100
16 - Pignose Amp (He used to put his harmonica)
17 - Echoplex EP-3 Tape Echo
18 - EMS Synth Hi-fli
19 - Roland Space Echo
20 - Eventide Harmonizer
21 - Lexicon DDL
22 - Roland Jazz Chorus 120
23 - Ernie Ball light 12 strings
24 - Fender 6 strings 0.10"
25 - Plastic pick-Fender medium

Signal Routing:

Gtr1/Gtr2 → Input selector → (Input Buffer) Peter Cornish LD-1 → Octivider → Duo Fuzz → Duo Fuzz Tone → Supa Tone Bender → Cry Baby → MXR Phase 90 →

MXR Phase 100 → Echo Send/Return (Echoplex EP-3 → Spare Send/Return → Master Effects Bypass → Schaller F121 Volume Pedal → (Preamp) Peter Cornish NB-3 → Output

from Steve Hackett - *Please Don't Touch*

How Can I?

by Steve Hackett

Transcribed by Paulo De Carvalho

♩=70

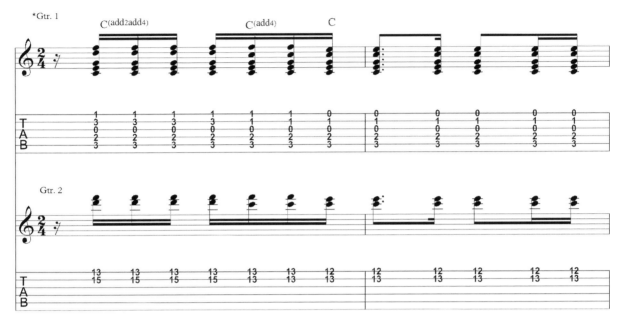

*Gtr. 1: Two 12 strings gtrs. arr. for one.

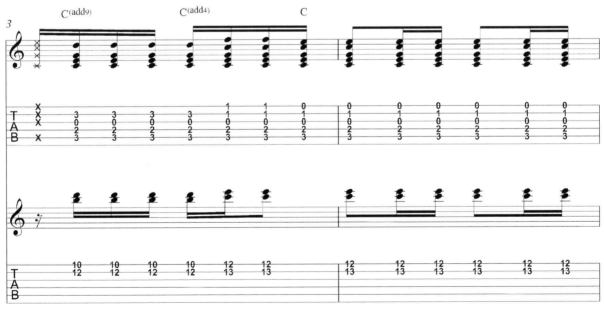

The lo-cal ra - dio__ says sor – ry time to go
The la-dy isn't_____ here The mes-sage wasn't_ clear

*Roland Synth GR 500: Polyensemble section set with the F, L and M slider at the halfway point, the H staying at zero.
On the Envelope Generator the attack was full up and the decay halfway, the sustain at zero.

**Gtr. 3: continue with same chords as Gtr 1 but with rhytm like Rhy. Fig. 3

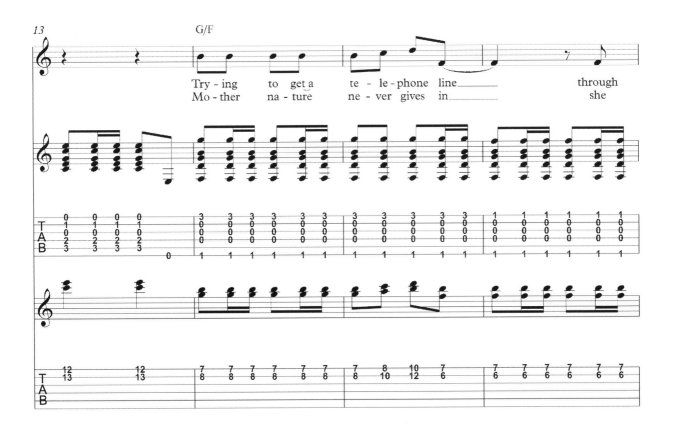

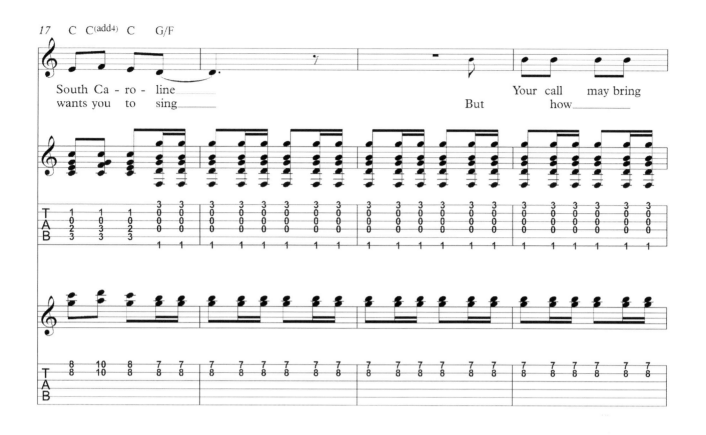

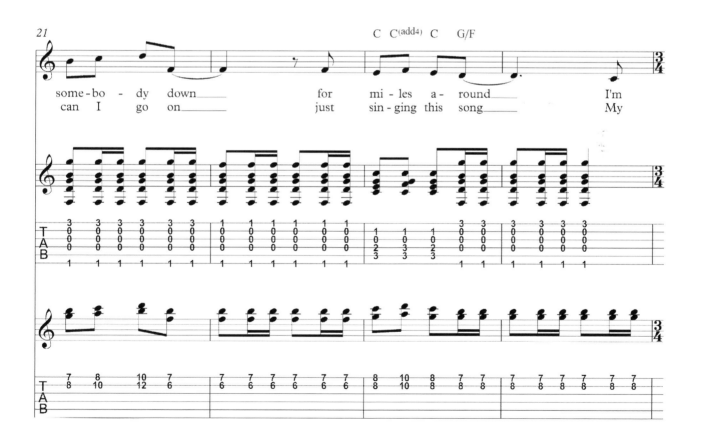

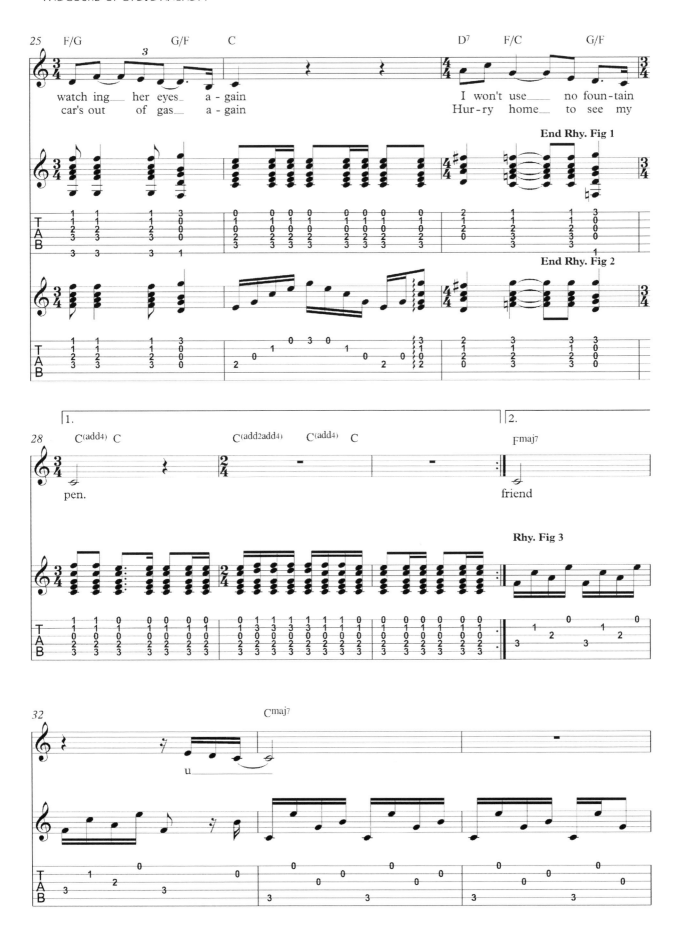

Gtr 1 w/ Rhy. Fig 1
Gtr 2 w/ Rhy. Fig 2

59   C   C(add2add4)   C(add4)   C

you   You must love some - one

63   C(add9)   C(add4)   C   C(add2add4)   C(add4)   C

else   or fa - ce life your - self   You may ex-pect a   call

68   C(add9)   C(add4)   C   G/F

She's wai ting__ in the hall__   See the gar - den grows and it grows

73   C   C(add4)   C   G/F

__ no - bo - dy else knows   And you can wear just

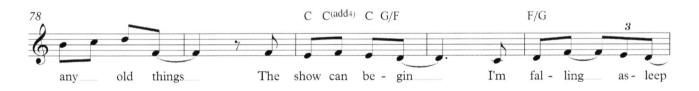

78   C   C(add4)   C   G/F   F/G   3

any old things__ The show can be - gin__ I'm fal - ling__ as - leep

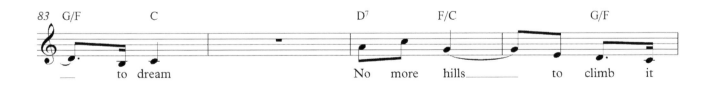

83   G/F   C   D7   F/C   G/F

__ to dream   No more hills__ to climb it

Gtr 1 w/ Rhy. Fig 3

D.S. al Coda

87 Fmaj7   3   Cmaj7   Fmaj7   Cmaj7

seems

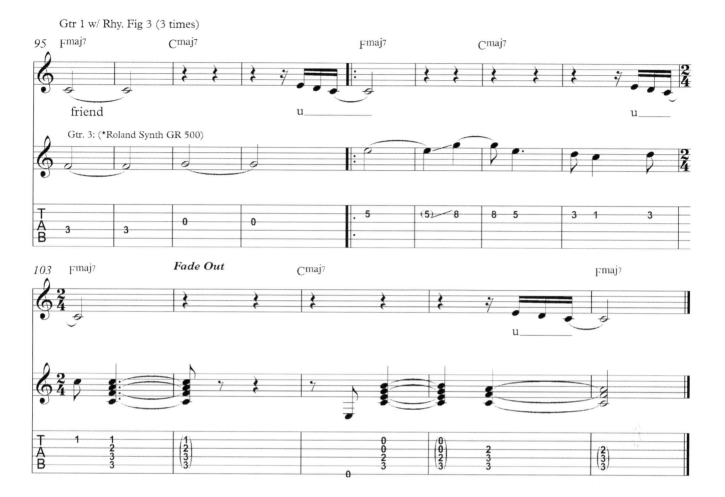

HOW CAN I?
BY STEVE HACKETT

Intro:
`|C(add2add4)  C(add4)  C  | C(add9)  C  |`

```
C(add2add4)    C(add4)  C     C(add9)                    C(add2add4) C
THE LOCAL   RADI - O     SAYS SORRY TIME    TO           GO
C(add2add4)           C(add4)  C
BUT I DON'T SLEEP TOO      WELL
C(add9)                   C(add2add4)  C
WHERE ARE THOSE SOUTHERN   BELLES
G/F
TRYIN' TO GET A TELEPHONE LINE
            C          C(add4) C  G/F
THROUGH SOUTH      CA - - ROLINA
G/F
YOUR CALL MAY BRING SOMEBODY DOWN
     C    C(add4) C G/F
FOR MILES      AROUND
      F/G              G/F      C
I'M WATCHING HER EYES AGAIN
D7       F/C      G/F          C(add2add4) C(add4)  C
I WON'T USE NO FOUNTAIN PEN
```

`|C(add2add4)  C(add4)  C`

```
C(add2add4) C(add4)  C      C(add9)        C(add2add4) C
THE LADY    ISN'T    HERE. THE MESSAGE WASN'T       CLEAR
C(add2add4)  C(add4)  C
SHE LEFT AN HOUR   AGO,
C(add9)                      C(add2add4)    C
SCREAMED FROM THE FLOOR  BE - - - - - - - LOW
G/F
MOTHER NATURE NEVER GIVES IN,
     C        C(add4)  C  G/F
SHE WANTS YOU   TO  SING BUT HOW CAN I GO ON
     C   C(add4) C    G/F
JUST SINGING   THIS SONG

    F/G             G/F      C
MY CAR'S OUT OF GAS AGAIN
D7       F/C        G/F     Fmaj7
HURRY HOME TO SEE MY FRIEND
```

`Cmaj7    |      |Fmaj7     |       | Cmaj7     |`

```
Am                D7/F#                G(sus4)  G
MONEY WON'T HELP YOU TO WIN
   C(add4)  C          G/F
A NEW    LOOK AT THINGS LOVING   CAN   BRING
         C        C (add4)   C   G/F
YOU DOWN SO        YOU FALL  THEN WHY DO YOU STILL TRY
      C     C (add4)  C  G/F
TO GET UP         AT ALL
            F/G                   G/F        C
YOUR GOOD AND BAD SIDE SHOWING THROUGH
D7            F/C     G/F        C(add2add4) C(add4)  C
PROBLEMS ARE A PART OF YOU


|C(add2add4)  C(add4)  C


C(add2add4)        C(add4)     C
YOU MUST LOVE SOMEONE ELSE
C(add9)              C(add4)  C
   OR FACE LIFE  BY YOURSELF
C(add2add4)   C(add4)    C      C(add9)        C(add4) C
YOU   MAY   EXPECT A CALL  SHE'S WAITING  IN THE  HALL
G/F
SEE THE GARDEN GROWS AND IT GROWS
      C  C(add4) C    G/F
NOBODY        ELSE KNOWS AND YOU CAN WEAR JUST ANY OLD THING
      C      C(add4) C  G/F
THE SHOW CAN   BEGIN
F/G            G/F          C
I'M FALLING ASLEEP    TO DREAM
D7          F/C      G/F       Fmaj7
NO MORE HILLS TO CLIMB IT SEEMS
Cmaj7   |    |Fmaj7    |     | Cmaj7     |


Am                D7/F#                G(sus4)  G
MONEY WON'T HELP YOU TO WIN
   C(add4)  C          G/F
A NEW  LOOK AT THINGS YOU NEVER GIVE IN
      C    C(add4) C        G/F
SO WHY DON'T   YOU SING
                        C   C (add4)  C    G/F
BUT HOW CAN I GO ON JUST SINGING    THIS SONG
      F/G            G/F      C
MY CAR'S OUT OF GAS AGAIN
D7       F/C      G/F     Fmaj7   Cmaj7
I'LL BE HOME TO SEE MY FRIEND
|Fmaj7    |     | Cmaj7     |        |  Repeat and fade out
```

THE SOUND OF STEVE HACKETT

SPECTRAL MORNINGS

This album was recorded at Phonogram Studios, Hilversum, The Netherlands, between the months of January and February 1979. It was released in May 1979.

This was Steve's third solo album and the first with his own band: Nick Magnus on keyboards, Vox string thing, novatron, clavichord, clavinet, Fender rhodes electric piano, Mini Moog and Roland string; Dik Cadbury on bass, Taurus Moog bass pedals and harmony/backing vocals; John Hackett on the flute, bamboo flute and Taurus Moog bass pedals; John Shearer on drums and percussion; Peter Hicks on vocals, and Suzanne Ciani on Modular synthesizer. Steve played acoustic and electric guitars, Roland guitar synth, harmonicas, koto on *The Red Flowers of Tachai Blooms Everywhere* and he sang back vocals. Steve sang lead vocals on *The Ballad of the Decomposing Man*.

SPECTRAL MORNINGS (THE SONG)

Spectral Mornings was initially conceived to have lyrics although it end it up being an instrumental track. Steve used a Gibson LesPaul Goldtop Guitar, a Roland GR with Ebow with a Tone Bender, an Echoplex and a Roland Jazz Chorus 120 with Chorus on. He doubled the guitar part as he did in *Every Day* in the same album.

The intro of the song using Roland GR, Ebow and a clean guitar in the chords created a "morning" atmosphere. Nowadays Steve no longer uses this intro in his concerts.

The fingerings I wrote are exactly the ones Steve used to play. The intro was built in E major and when the melody began, the song was in D Major. The chords in the beginning of the theme were: D/A G(add9)/B A(add9)/C#, in which the same hand shape of G(add9)/B moved up two frets to make the A(dd9)/C#.

Studio Gears : Spectral Mornings (Jan-Feb 1979)

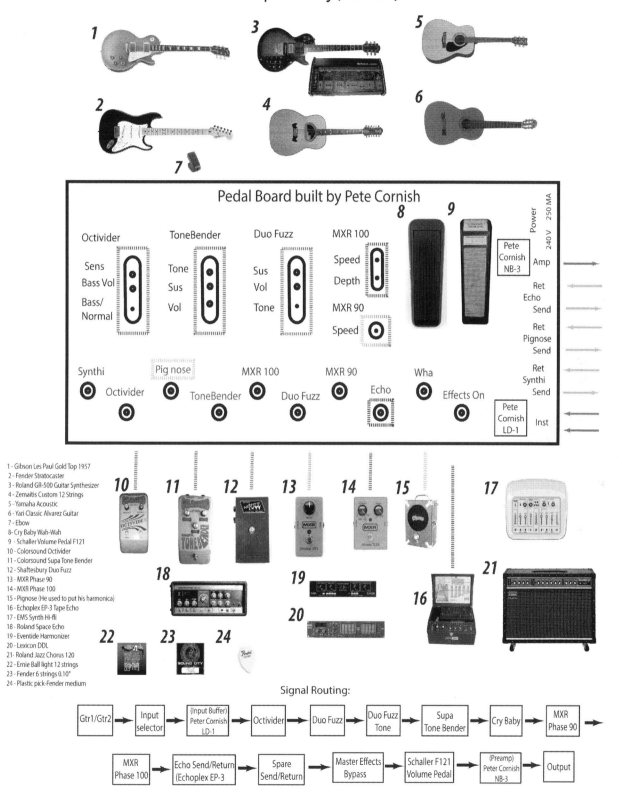

Pedal Board built by Pete Cornish

1 - Gibson Les Paul Gold Top 1957
2 - Fender Stratocaster
3 - Roland GR-500 Guitar Synthesizer
4 - Zemaitis Custom 12 Strings
5 - Yamaha Acoustic
6 - Yari Classic Alvarez Guitar
7 - Ebow
8 - Cry Baby Wah-Wah
9 - Schaller Volume Pedal F121
10 - Colorsound Octivider
11 - Colorsound Supa Tone Bender
12 - Shaftesbury Duo Fuzz
13 - MXR Phase 90
14 - MXR Phase 100
15 - Pignose (He used to put his harmonica)
16 - Echoplex EP-3 Tape Echo
17 - EMS Synth Hi-fli
18 - Roland Space Echo
19 - Eventide Harmonizer
20 - Lexicon DDL
21 - Roland Jazz Chorus 120
22 - Ernie Ball light 12 strings
23 - Fender 6 strings 0.10"
24 - Plastic pick-Fender medium

Signal Routing:

Gtr1/Gtr2 → Input selector → (Input Buffer) Peter Cornish LD-1 → Octivider → Duo Fuzz → Duo Fuzz Tone → Supa Tone Bender → Cry Baby → MXR Phase 90

MXR Phase 100 → Echo Send/Return (Echoplex EP-3) → Spare Send/Return → Master Effects Bypass → Schaller F121 Volume Pedal → (Preamp) Peter Cornish NB-3 → Output

from Steve Hackett - *Spectral Mornings*

Spectral Mornings

by Steve Hackett

Transcribed by Paulo De Carvalho

♩ = 70

Intro

*Gtr. 1 Guitar Roland GR with Ebow

**Gtr. 2 tcl. and gtr arr. for 1 gtr.

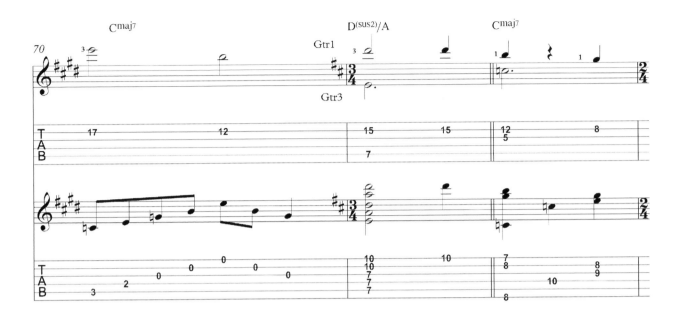

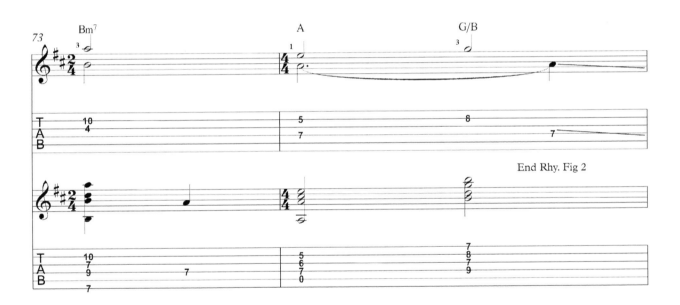

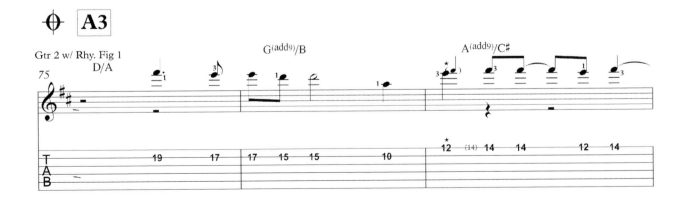

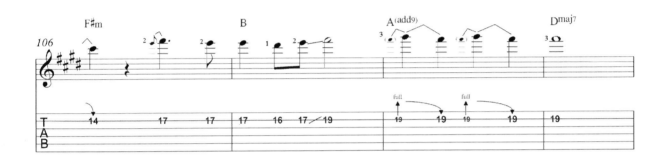

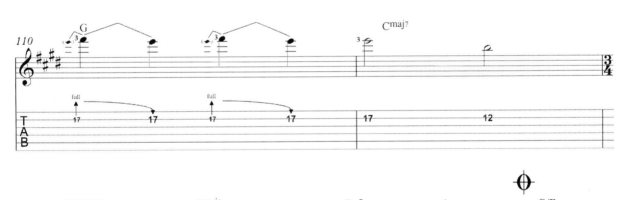

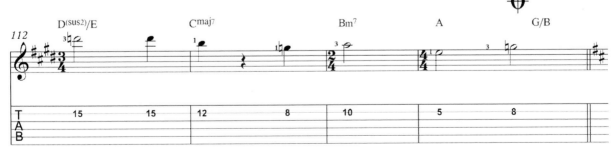

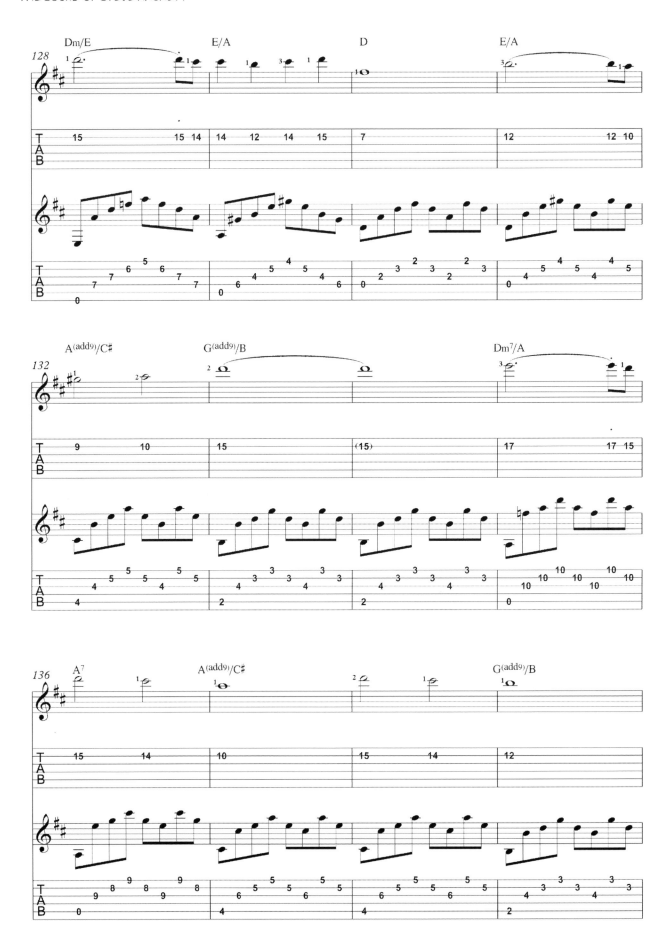

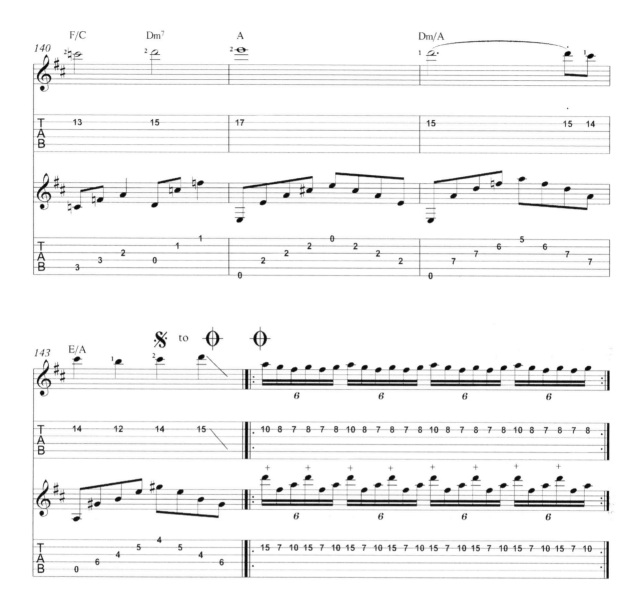

DEFECTOR

Defector was recorded at Wessex Sound in England in the Spring of 1980. It was released in June 1980.

THE STEPPES

Steve named *The Steppes* after a made-up journey to land masses. It has nuances when there are chord changes between E and B/E, with a melody line that blends gracefully with the chords.

The use of different guitars and keyboard in the melody created a harmony that contrasts with the strong drums.

On the E major chord on bar 18, Steve played a melody on the E minor harmonic scale (E F# G A B C D#).

On bar 62, he played the B major scale until bar 72, when he went back to the E minor harmonic scale.

For this track Steve used a Fender Stratocaster.

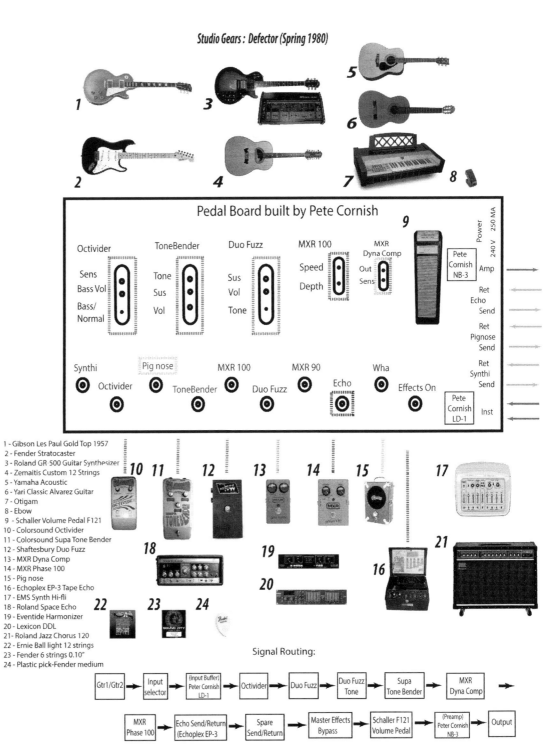

Studio Gears : Defector (Spring 1980)

Pedal Board built by Pete Cornish

1 - Gibson Les Paul Gold Top 1957
2 - Fender Stratocaster
3 - Roland GR-500 Guitar Synthesizer
4 - Zemaitis Custom 12 Strings
5 - Yamaha Acoustic
6 - Yari Classic Alvarez Guitar
7 - Otigam
8 - Ebow
9 - Schaller Volume Pedal F121
10 - Colorsound Octivider
11 - Colorsound Supa Tone Bender
12 - Shaftesbury Duo Fuzz
13 - MXR Dyna Comp
14 - MXR Phase 100
15 - Pig nose
16 - Echoplex EP-3 Tape Echo
17 - EMS Synth Hi-fli
18 - Roland Space Echo
19 - Eventide Harmonizer
20 - Lexicon DDL
21 - Roland Jazz Chorus 120
22 - Ernie Ball light 12 strings
23 - Fender 6 strings 0.10"
24 - Plastic pick-Fender medium

Signal Routing:

Gtr1/Gtr2 → Input selector → (Input Buffer) Peter Cornish LD-1 → Octivider → Duo Fuzz → Duo Fuzz Tone → Supa Tone Bender → MXR Dyna Comp →

MXR Phase 100 → Echo Send/Return (Echoplex EP-3 → Spare Send/Return → Master Effects Bypass → Schaller F121 Volume Pedal → (Preamp) Peter Cornish NB-3 → Output

from Steve Hackett - *Defector*
The Steppes
by Steve Hackett

Transcribed by Paulo De Carvalho

♩ = 58

ad libitum

*Gtr. 1 winds, tcl. and gtr arr. for 1 gtr.

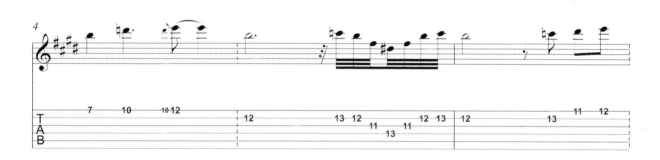

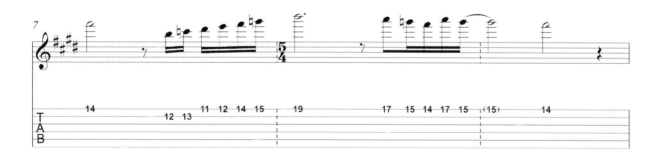

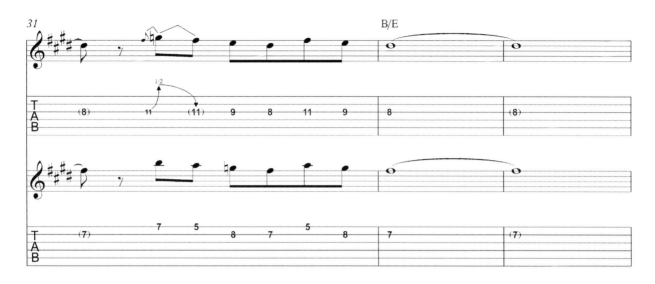

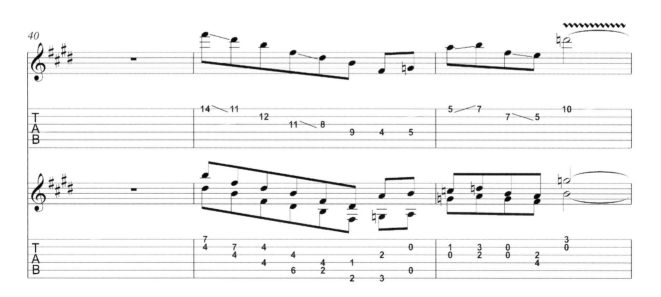

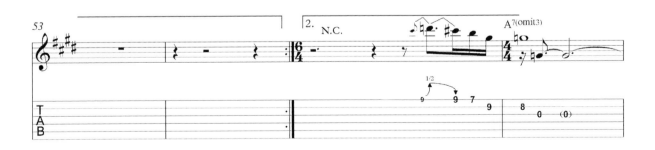

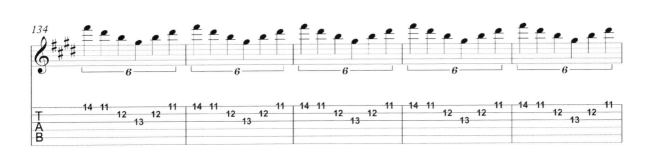

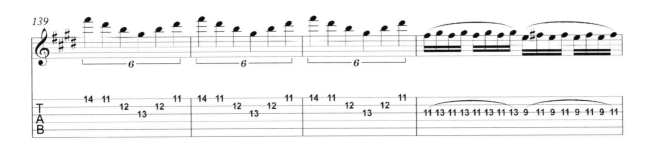

BAY OF KINGS

This album was recorded between 1980 and 1983. It was released in October 1983.

Bay of Kings was the first in a sequence of Steve's prominent albums for classical guitar.

Steve's record company at the time didn't show interest in the album. Lamborghini Records, an independent record company, was the one that ended it up releasing it.

BLACK LIGHT

Steve composed *Black Light* in an *etude* style, using chord changes in triplets in a continuous movement of the right hand. All triplets used *p i m*. It is in the key of Am with the B section in A major.

The chords are: Am G6 Em C Fmaj7/A Fmaj7(b5)/A E7 E7/G# and then back to Am. In the repeat of the section, instead of going to Am, it goes to A major E7. From bar 26 until 36 Steve used P i m i.

Studio Gears : Bay of Kings (1983)

Yairi Nylon Alvarez

from Steve Hackett - *Bay of Kings*

Black Light

by Steve Hackett

Transcribed by Paulo De Carvalho

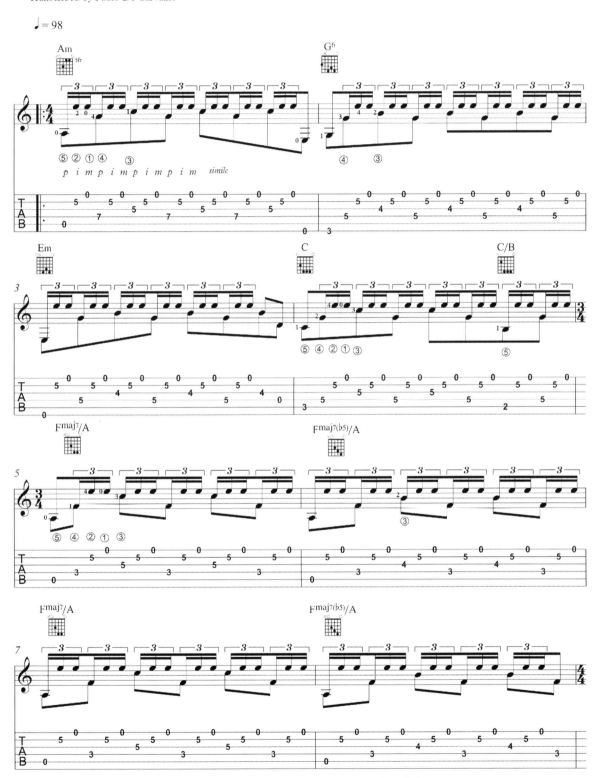

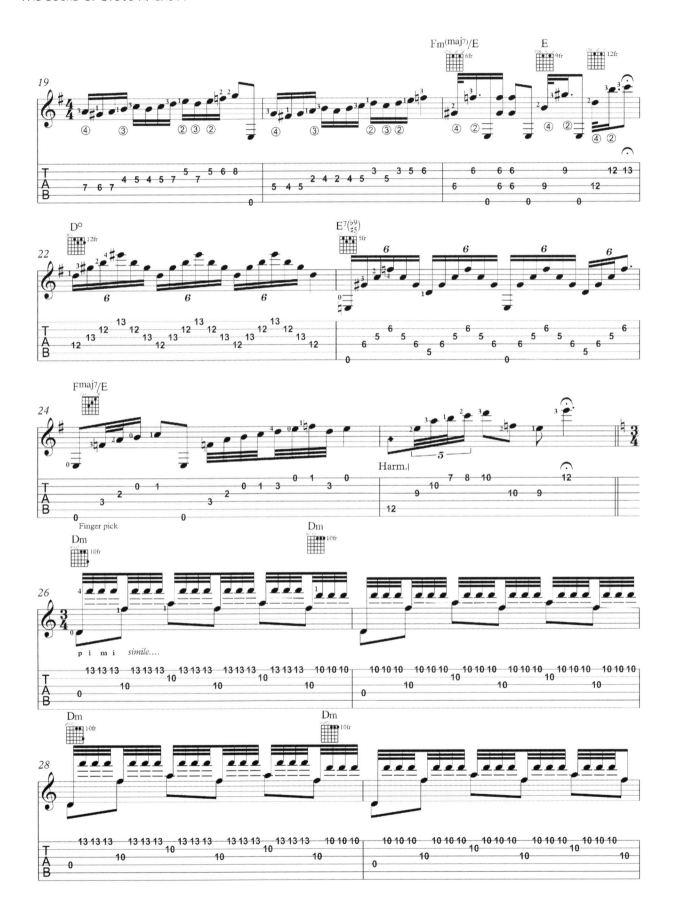

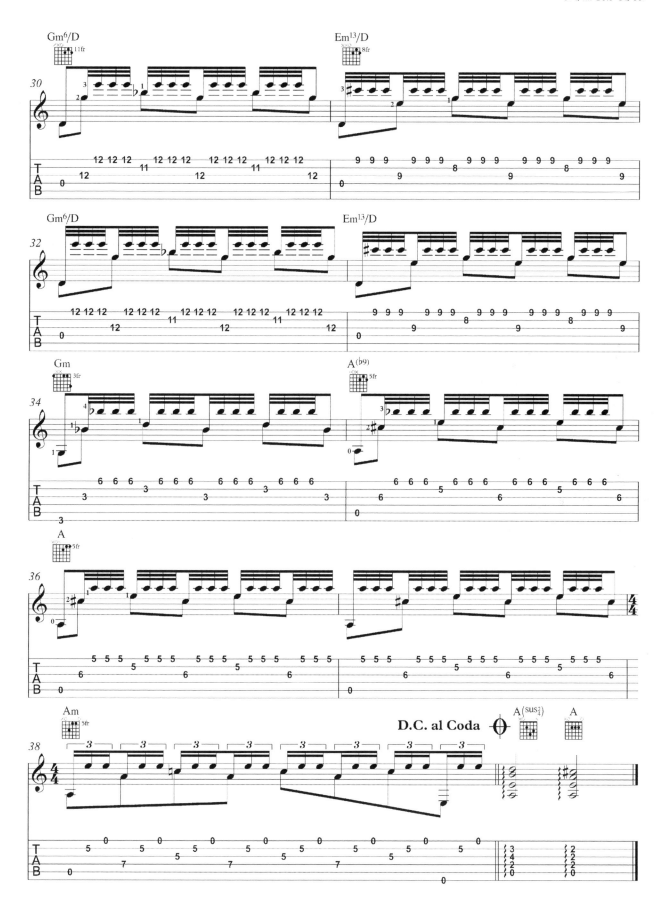

MOMENTUM

An acoustic album, *Momentum* started to be recorded in 1987, being completed and released in the following year. It was a contrasting album to its previous one, *GTR*, a rock album recorded in 1986 with the super group GTR which included Steve Howe.

Momentum featured only Steve, on the acoustic guitar and keyboards, and John Hackett, on the flute.

THE SLEEPING SEA

In *The Sleeping Sea*, the 6th string must be tuned in D, instead of in E, in order for this piece, in Dm, to have a deeper sonority.

The superb chord sequence Dm   Cm/D   Dm   Dm/F   Gm/A creates a perfect atmosphere to play the song with different nuances.

The B section is in D major with the sequence: D   Gm/D   Ebmaj7   D   D7(b9). On measures 25 and 26, D goes to Dm without preparation, and the song finishes in the key of Dm.

Studio Gears : Momentum (1988)

Yairi Nylon Alvarez

from Steve Hackett - *Momentum*

The Sleeping Sea

by Steve Hackett

Transcribed by Paulo De Carvalho

(low to high) D-A-D-G-B-E

♩ = 60

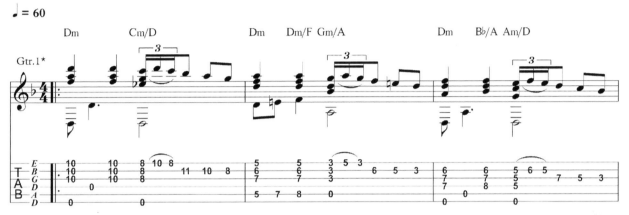

Gtr.1* (Nylon-str. acous.)

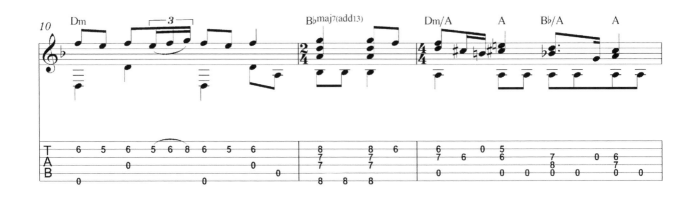

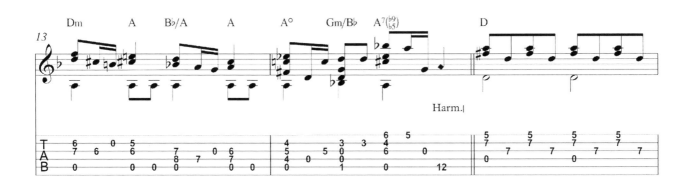

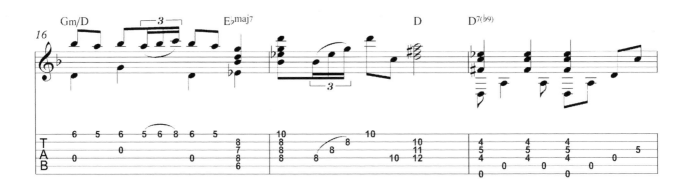

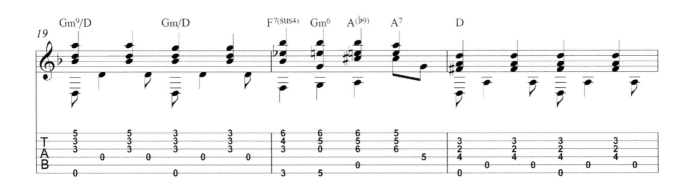

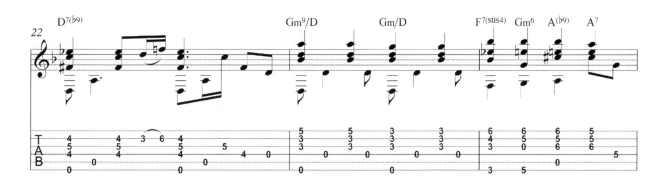

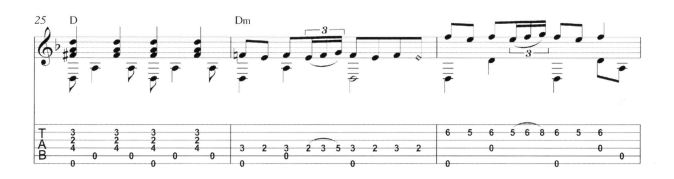

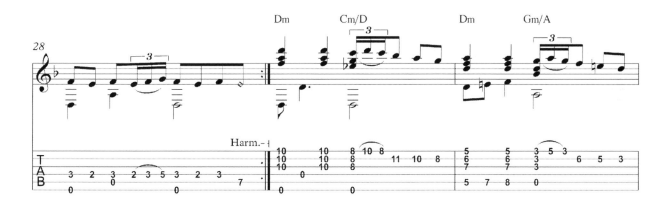

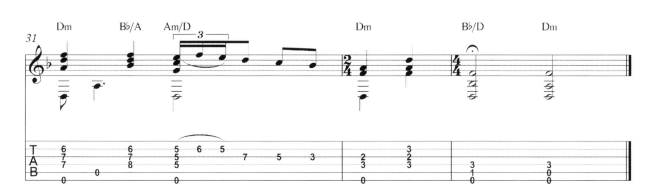

A MIDSUMMER NIGHT'S DREAM

A *Midsummer Night's Dream* was recorded and released in 1997.

Steve wrote the album inspired by Shakespeare's *Midsummer Night's Dream*. For few months it was on the list of best classical albums.

He played the acoustic guitar along with John Hackett, Roger King and The Royal Philharmonic Orchestra.

TITANIA

This song was inspired by the Queen of the Fairies *Titania*, a strong and proud creature .

Originally written for classical guitar, *Titania* is an ideal tune to practice different techniques. It begins with the Bm9(b6) chord, but you can also interpret it as an Em9/B. Then it goes to A7, Bm6, C#m, A7, D, Gmaj7, C#m7(b9), and Bm. In order to play this song, the guitar player has to always let the note ring until the next chord is heard.

Studio Gears : Midsummer (1997)

Yairi Nylon Alvarez

from Steve Hackett - *A Midsummer Night's Dream*

Titania

by Steve Hackett

Transcribed by Paulo De Carvalho

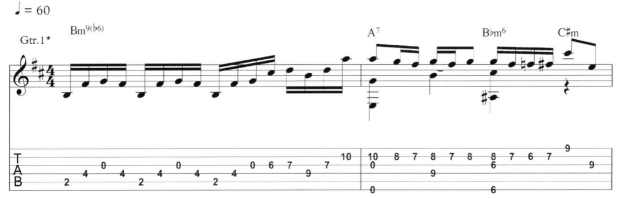

Gtr.1* (Nylon-str. acous.)

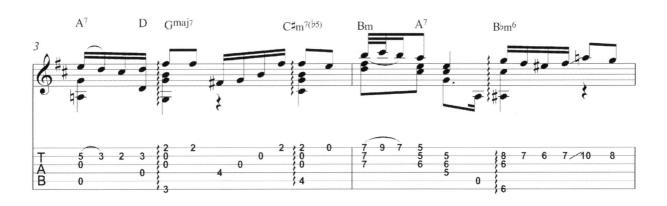

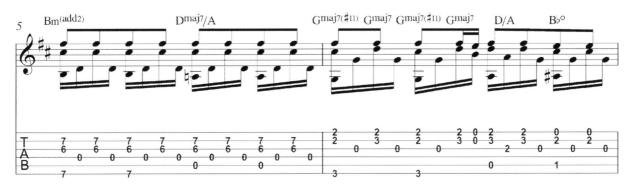

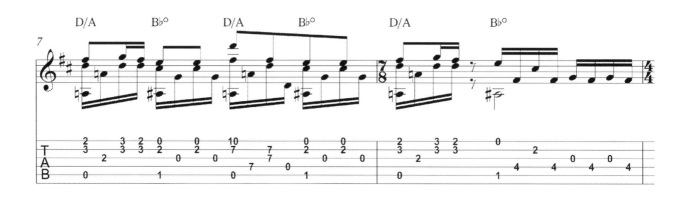

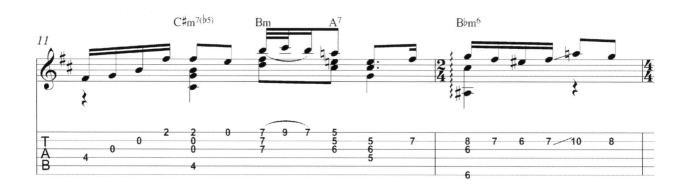

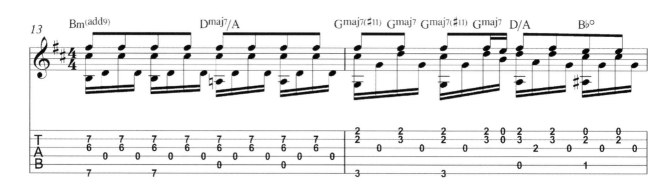

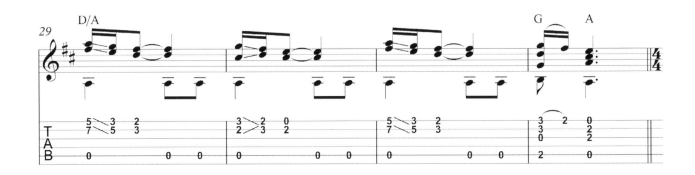

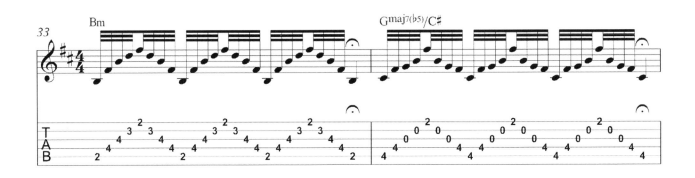

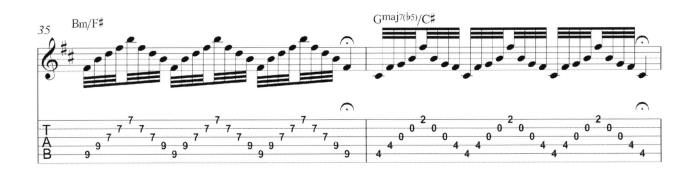

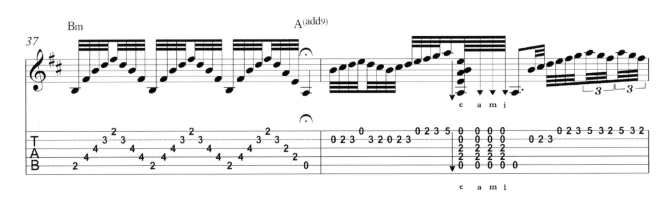

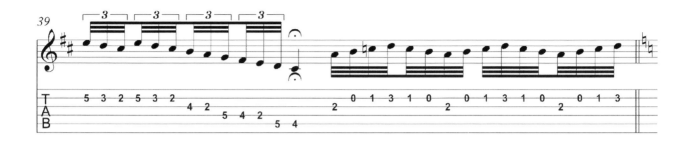

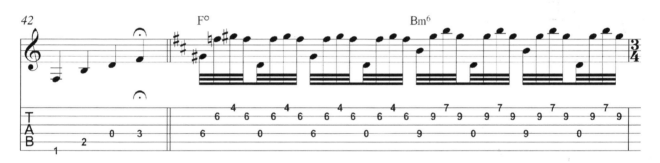

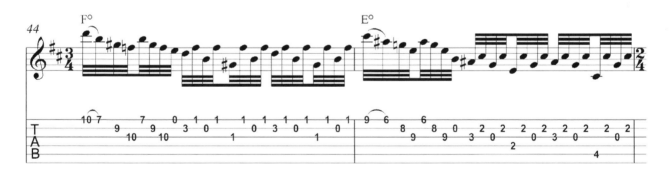

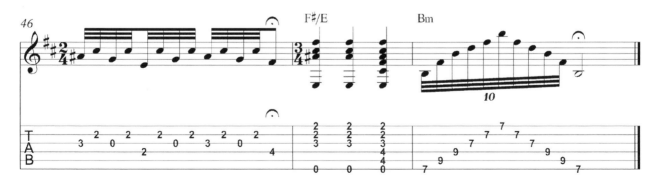

LIVE RAILS

Live Rails was recorded live between 2009 and 2010 on tours to Paris, London and New York.

ACE OF WANDS

This song was, at first, the opening track of *Voyage of the Acolyte*. Therefore it was recorded in 1975 in studio with Steve using a Les Paul Guitar, H&H overdriven amp with the melody played in octaves, Fender Champ with Echoplex, Colorsound Fuzz box and Shaftesbury DuoFuzz - both used in series, plus an acoustic Yamaha guitar recorded at half speed and reversed with repeat echo. For the final phrases Steve used an MXR Phase 90.

At the *Live Rails* concerts, Steve played *Ace of Wands* with a Fernandes Black 2005.

Live Gears : Live Rails (2011)

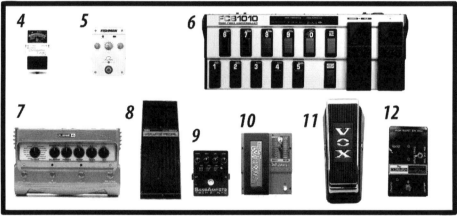

1 - Fernandes Black 2005
2 - Zemaitis 12 strings
3 - Yairi nylon strings
4 - Boss Tuner
5 - Fishmans Aura Acoustic
6 - Behringer FCB 1010 Midi Controler
7 - Line 6 Delay Modeler
8 - Volume Pedal
9 - San Amp GT2
10 - Digitech Whammy 4
15 - Cry Baby Wah
16 - Peter Cornish Iron Booster
18 - Marshall Head 1987x
19 - Marshall 1960A Cab

from Steve Hackett - *Live Rails*

Ace of Wands

by Steve Hackett

Transcribed by Paulo De Carvalho

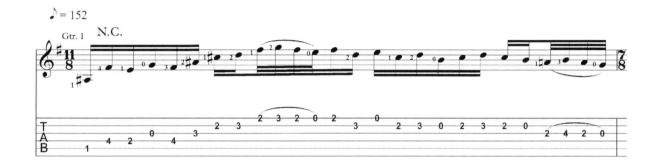

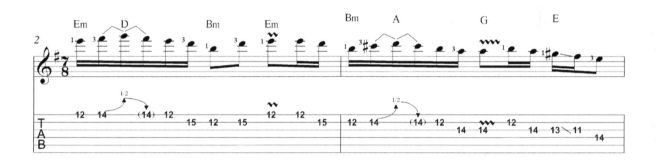

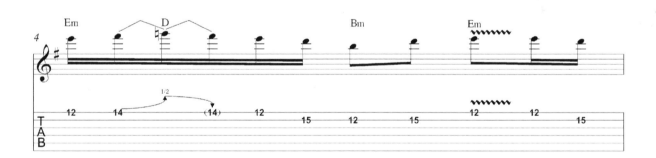

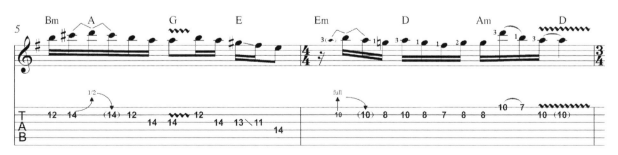

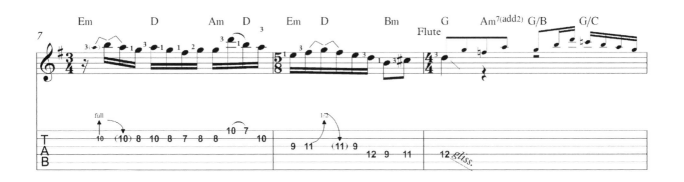

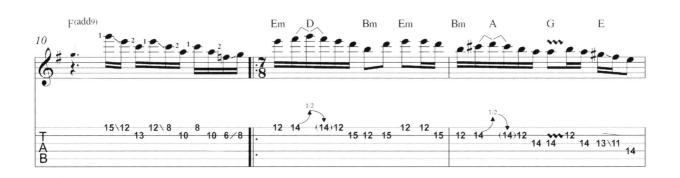

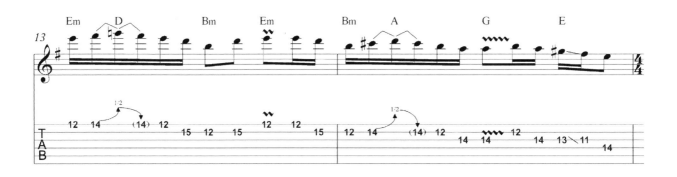

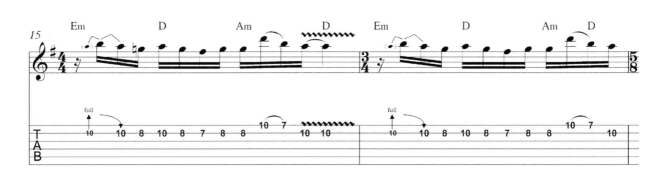

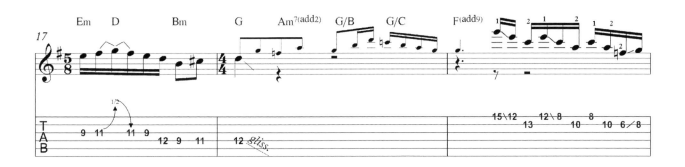

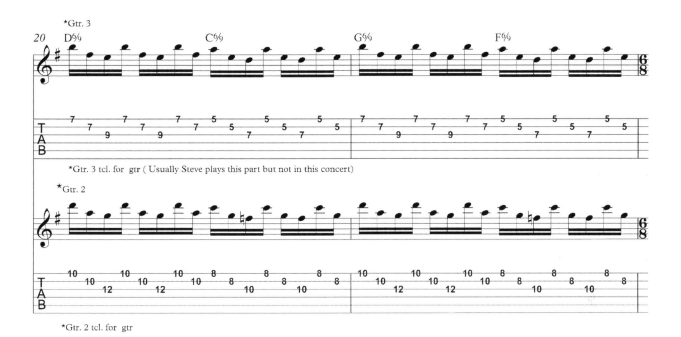

*Gtr. 3 tcl. for gtr (Usually Steve plays this part but not in this concert)

*Gtr. 2 tcl. for gtr

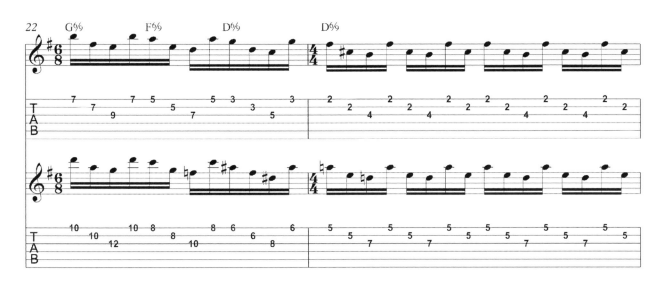

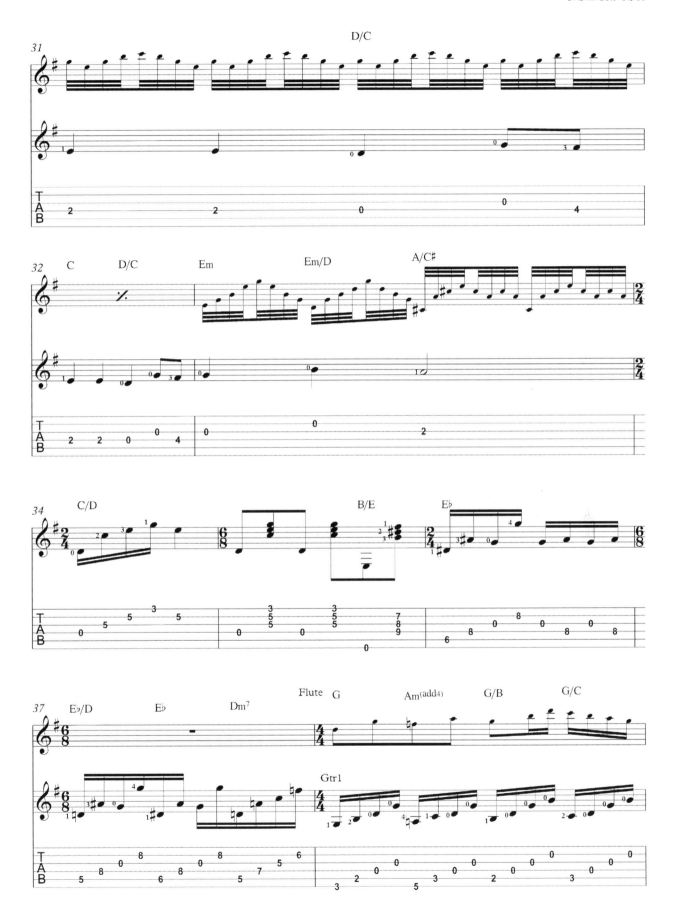

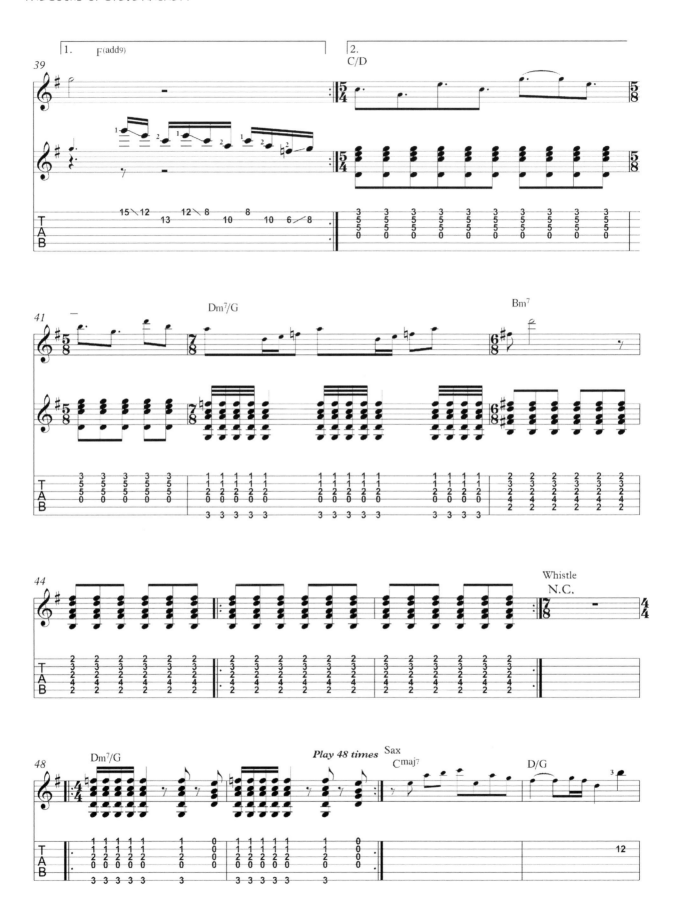

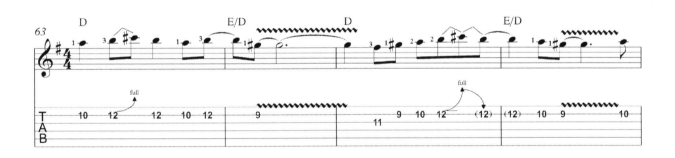

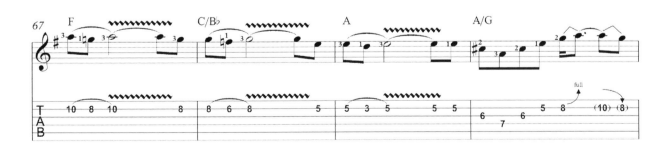

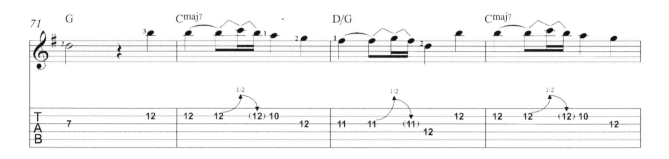

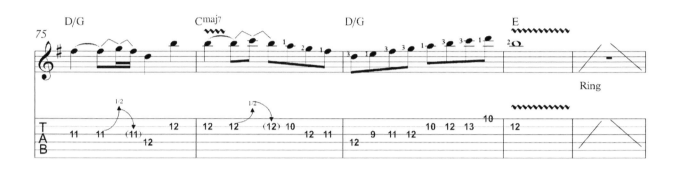

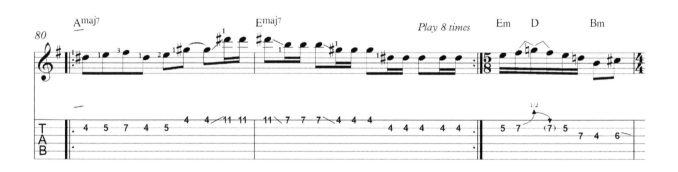

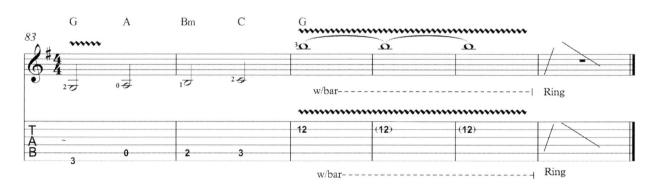

GENESIS REVISITED II

Genesis Revisited II was recorded between 2011 and 2012. It was released in October 2012.

A TOWER STRUCK DOWN

Like *Ace of Wands*, *A Tower Struck Down* was originally part of the 1975 album *Voyage of the Acolyte*. Steve used an EMS Synthi HiFli and a Gibson Les Paul Goldtop for this track.

As per *Ace of Wands* in the album *Live Rails*, Steve also played *A Tower Struck Down* with a Fernandes (Goldtop) in *Genesis Revisited II.*

Studio Gears: Genesis Revisited II (2012)

1 - Fernandes Gold Top
2 - Gibson Lespaul Top 1957
3 - Zemaitis 12 Strings
4 - Yairi Steel-strings 1974
5 - Rickenbacker 6 strings
6 - Line 6 DL4 Delay Modeler
7 - Korg KVP-002 Volume Pedal
8 - SansAmp GT2 Tech 21
9 - DigiTech Whammy
10 - Vox Wah V847
11 - Pete Cornish treble booster
12 - Marshall Head 1987x
13 - Marshall 1960A cabs
- Apple Logic amp simulators
- Amplitube III

from Steve Hackett - *Genesis Revisited II*

A Tower Struck Down

by Steve Hackett, John Hackett

Transcribed by Paulo De Carvalho

♩ = 116

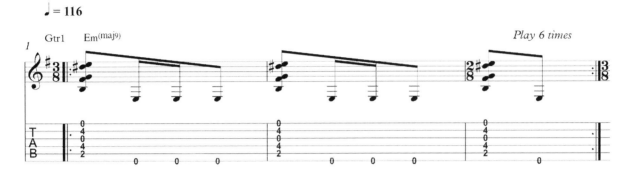

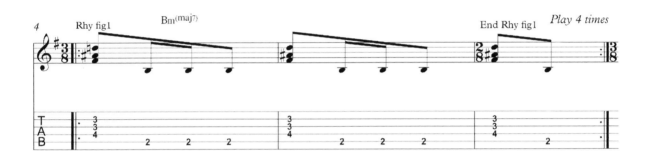

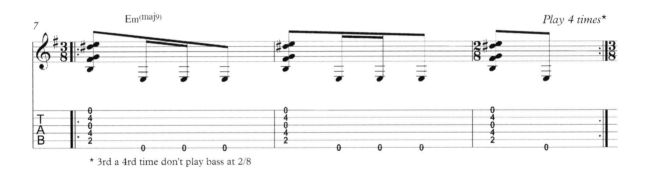

* 3rd a 4rd time don't play bass at 2/8

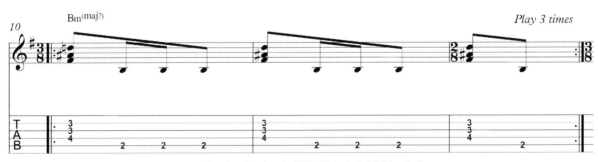

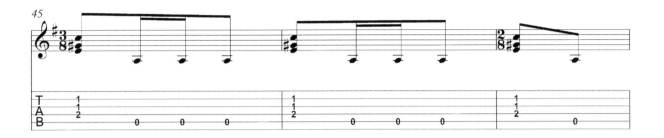

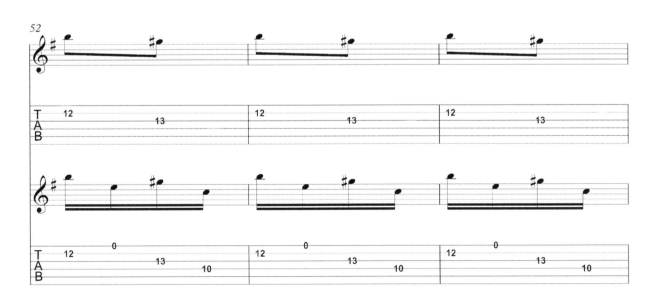

GENESIS REVISITED: LIVE AT HAMMERSMITH

Live at Hammersmith was recorded on May 10th, 2013. It was released as a CD/DVD album in November 2013. This tour was a great success, and it was based on the album *Genesis Revisited*, focusing on songs from Genesis.

This concert included: Steve on guitars and vocals; Roger King on keyboards; Garu O'Toole on drums, percussion and vocals; Rob Townsend on sax, flute and percussion; Lee Pomeroy on bass, and Nad Sylvan on vocals. It featured Amanda Lehmann on the guitar and vocals in the song *Shadow of the Hierophant*.

SHADOW OF THE HIEROPHANT

Shadow of the Hierophant was composed in partnership with Mike Rutherford. Part of the song was rehearsed with Genesis, but they never recorded it.

As *Ace of Wands* and *A Tower Struck* Down, this song was originally written in 1975 and it was part of the first solo album *Voyage of the Acolyte*.

SHADOW OF THE HIEROPHANT - 1975 VERSION
(ALBUM VOYAGE OF THE ACOLYTE)

On the 1975 version, in the beginning of the song, Steve used a Gibson Les Paul Goldtop with a slide on his little finger, using Tone Bender, an Echoplex and Volume Pedal.

In the later part of the song, he used a Tone Bender and Duo Fuzz together with Echoplex and MXR Phase 90 on slow setting.

The original singer was Mike Oldfield's sister, Sally Oldfield.

Steve played measures 10 through 33 with a different tuning as showed in the next two pages.

This is Steve's 1975 recording in G Major

Shadow Of The Hierophant

Steve Hackett/Mike Rutherford

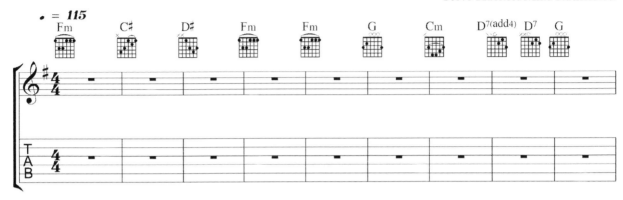

Tuning (low to high) E-A-D-G-B-D

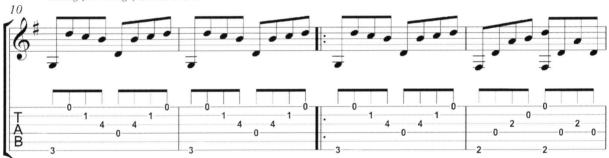

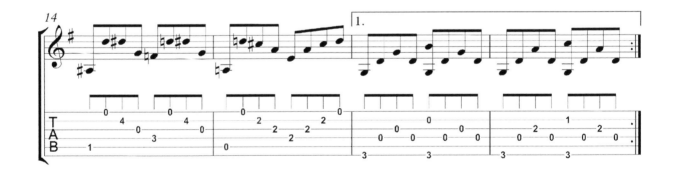

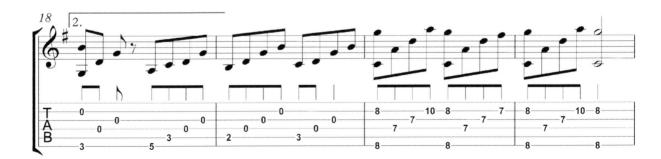

2

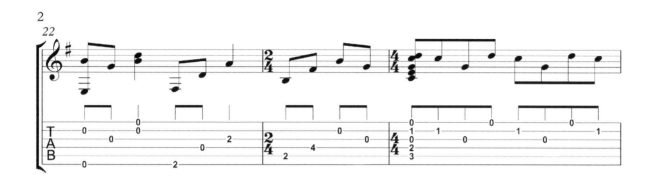

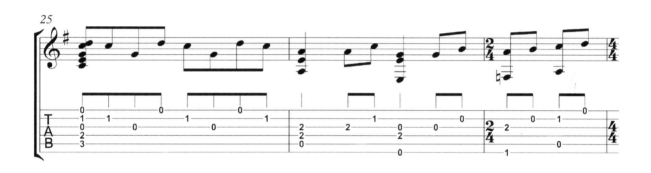

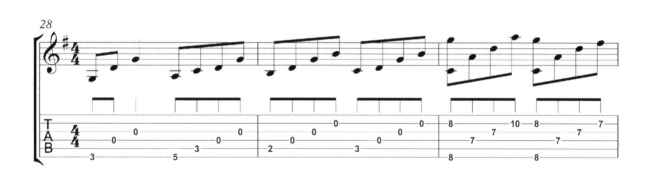

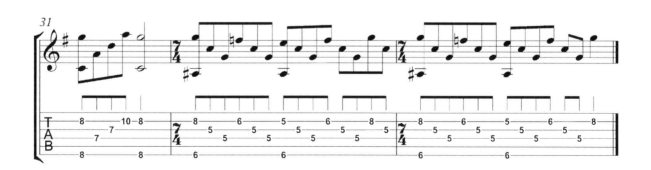

SHADOW OF THE HIEROPHANT - 2013 VERSION
(ALBUM GENESIS REVISITED: LIVE AT HAMMERSMITH)

For the 2013 live concerts of *Shadow of the Hierophant*, Steve used a Fernandes Goldtop with Line 6 Distortion Modeler to simulate the Fuzz pedals, and Line 6 Delay Modeler to simulate Echoplex, besides the SamAmp GT2. Amanda Lehmann sang and played the guitar.

Amanda used an Ibanez JS series guitar with a Boss GT10 guitar effect processor. She programmed a light chorus and compression for the picking and arpeggio fills between the verses and the later sequence that comes after the ample tapping. For the lead guitar, she programmed overdrive along with plenty of delay for a "big" sound, and continued to use this patch for the later power chord sequence, which provided a substantial sound that cuts through and powers on alongside the bass pedals.

In this version Steve changed the key on the start of the song to F Major and Roger King played the keyboard one step below to better match Amanda's voice.

Amanda stressed that, as she sang, she visualized a young woman with long dark hair, in a flowing white dress. The scenario was a shimmering lakeside in an emerald green forest, where the girl was waiting for her lover.

Because of that, at the beginning of the song she sang with a very young, innocent voice which, for her, illustrated the innocence of the girl. Amanda testified that as the years went by she sang the song naturally with a stronger voice, not losing the innocence and youth, but with a little more power and edge to it as if the character has grown up.

For Amanda, the song portrayed some sadness, especially in the last verse "tears fill the fountain, breaking their promise to heal". In her view, it is a song full of longing, beauty, innocence and pathos, and she has always tried to reflect that in her singing.

Live Gears : Live at Hammersmith, Live in Liverpool (2013-2016)

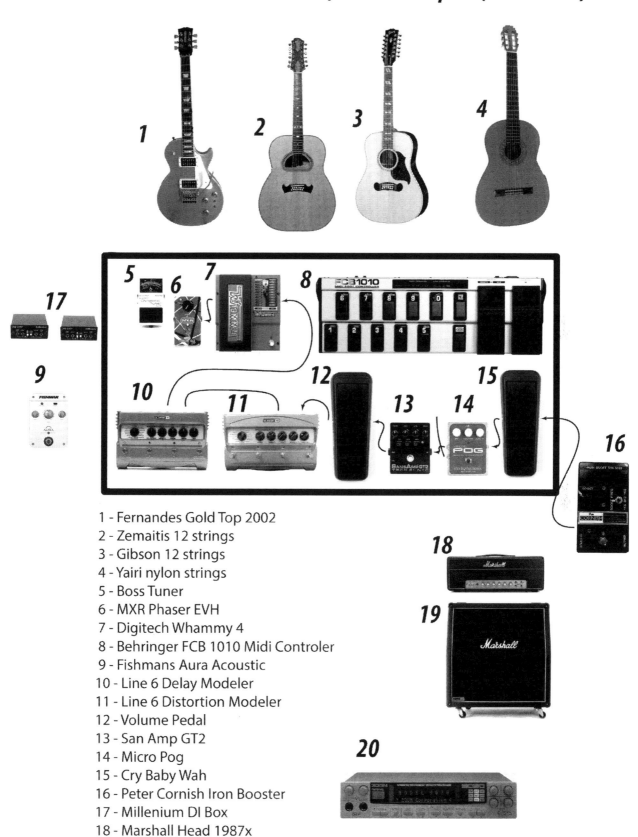

1 - Fernandes Gold Top 2002
2 - Zemaitis 12 strings
3 - Gibson 12 strings
4 - Yairi nylon strings
5 - Boss Tuner
6 - MXR Phaser EVH
7 - Digitech Whammy 4
8 - Behringer FCB 1010 Midi Controler
9 - Fishmans Aura Acoustic
10 - Line 6 Delay Modeler
11 - Line 6 Distortion Modeler
12 - Volume Pedal
13 - San Amp GT2
14 - Micro Pog
15 - Cry Baby Wah
16 - Peter Cornish Iron Booster
17 - Millenium DI Box
18 - Marshall Head 1987x
19 - Marshall 1960A Cab
20 - Zoom 9030

from Steve Hackett - *Genesis Revisited: Live at Hammersmith*

Shadow Of The Hierophant

by Steve Hackett, Mike Rutherford

Transcribed by Paulo De Carvalho

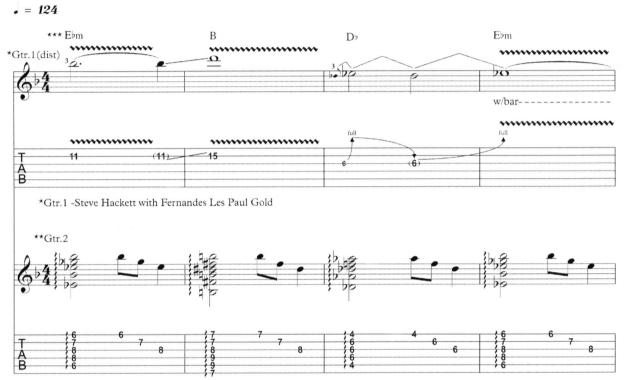

*Gtr.1 -Steve Hackett with Fernandes Les Paul Gold

**Gtr2 - Amanda Lehmann with Ibanez JS series

***Chords symbols reflect implied harmony

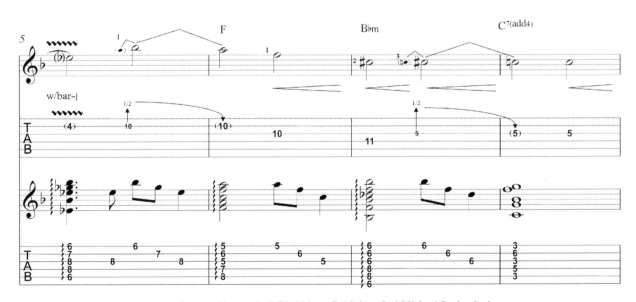

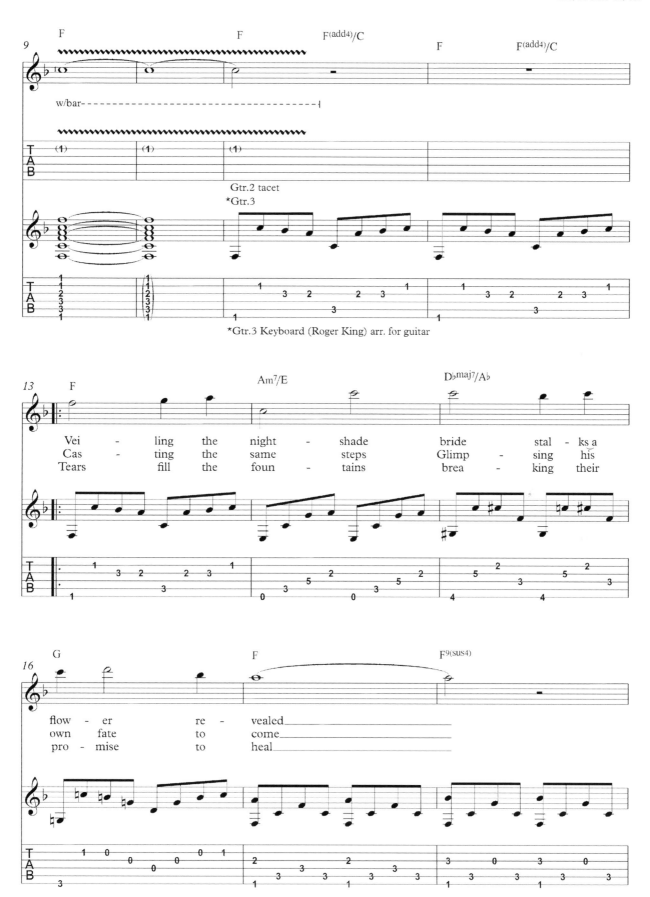

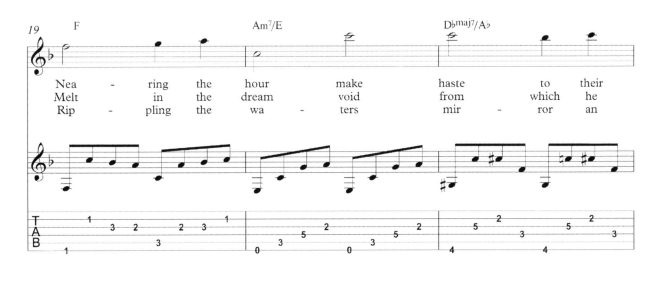

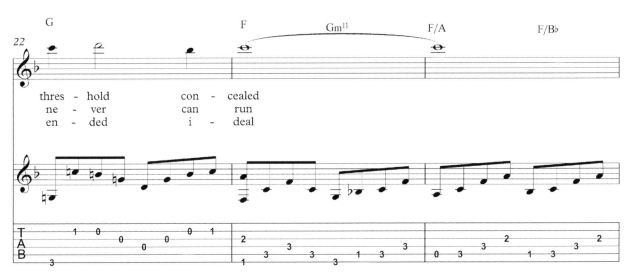

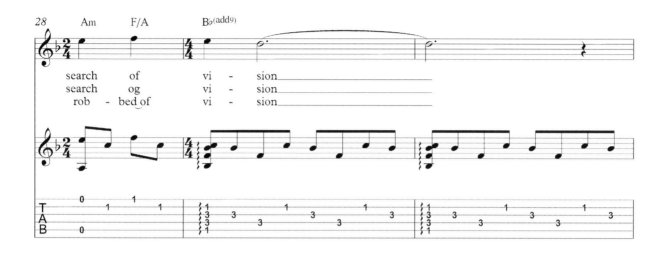

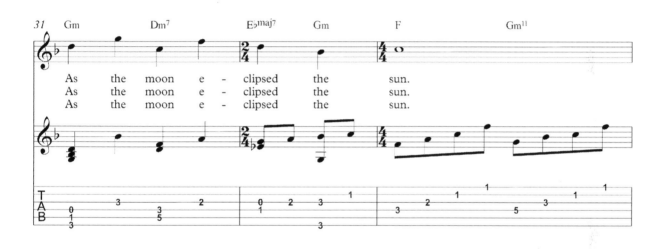

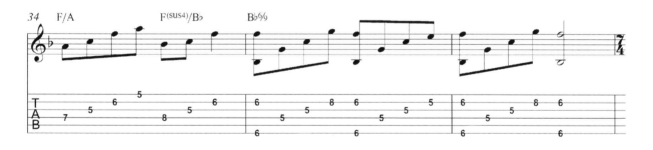

D.C. 2 times to ⊕ Coda

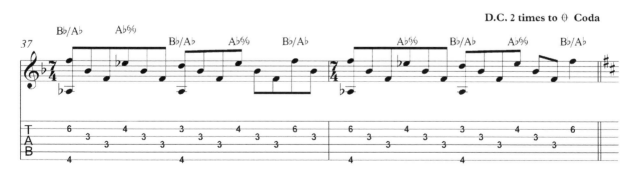

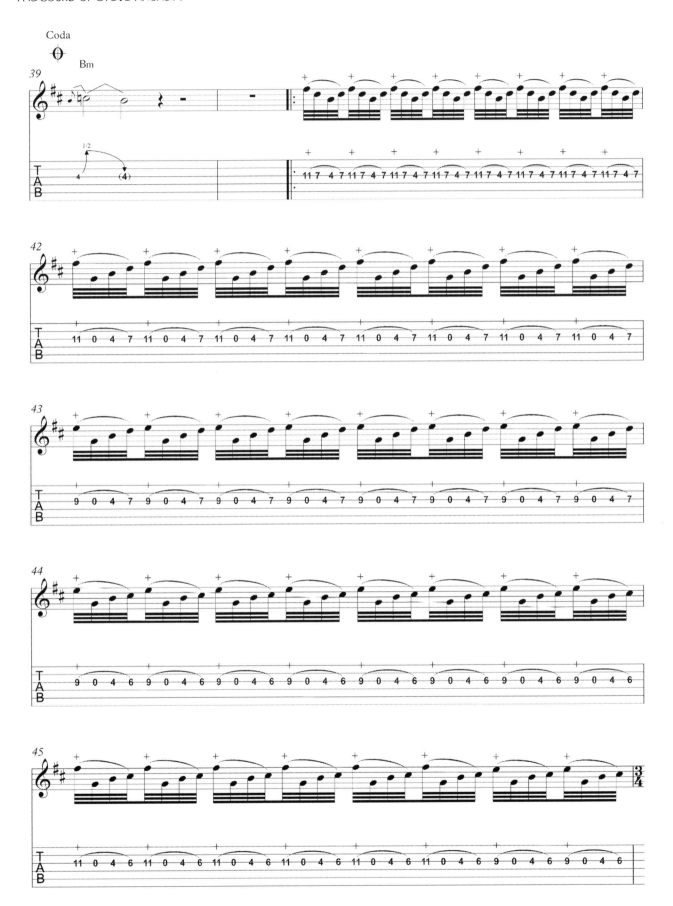

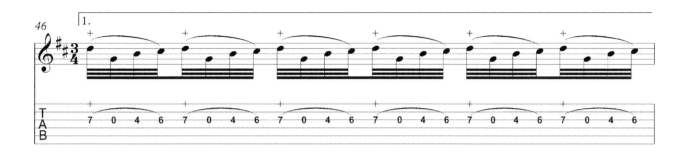

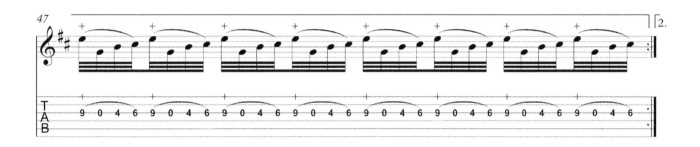

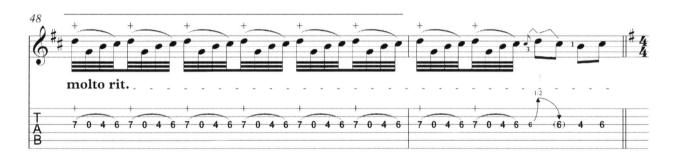

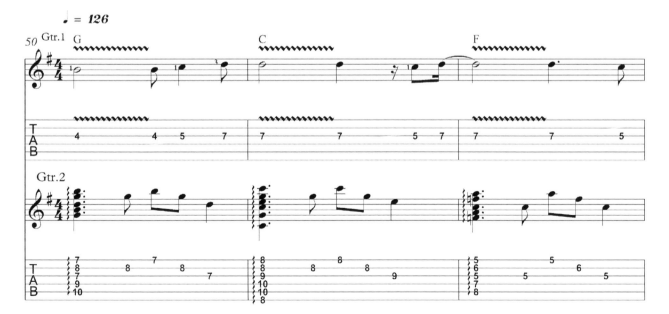

111

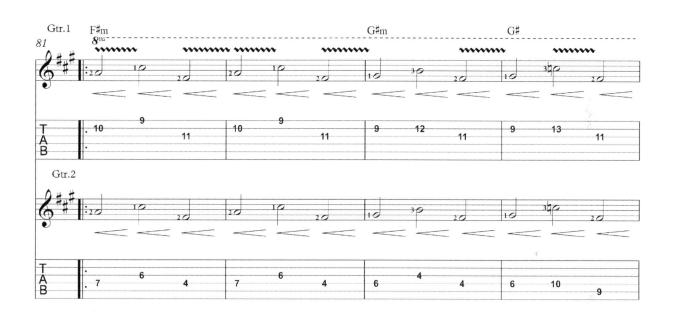

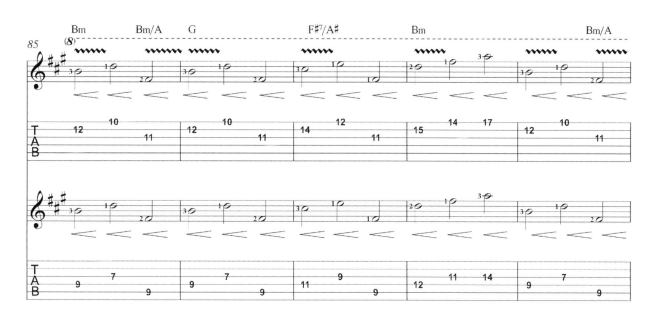

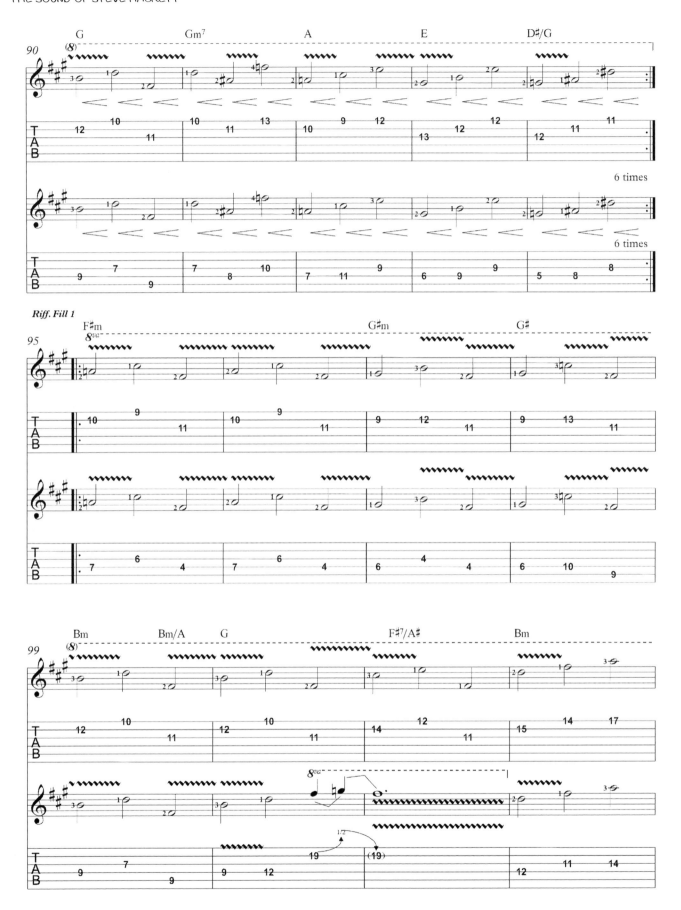

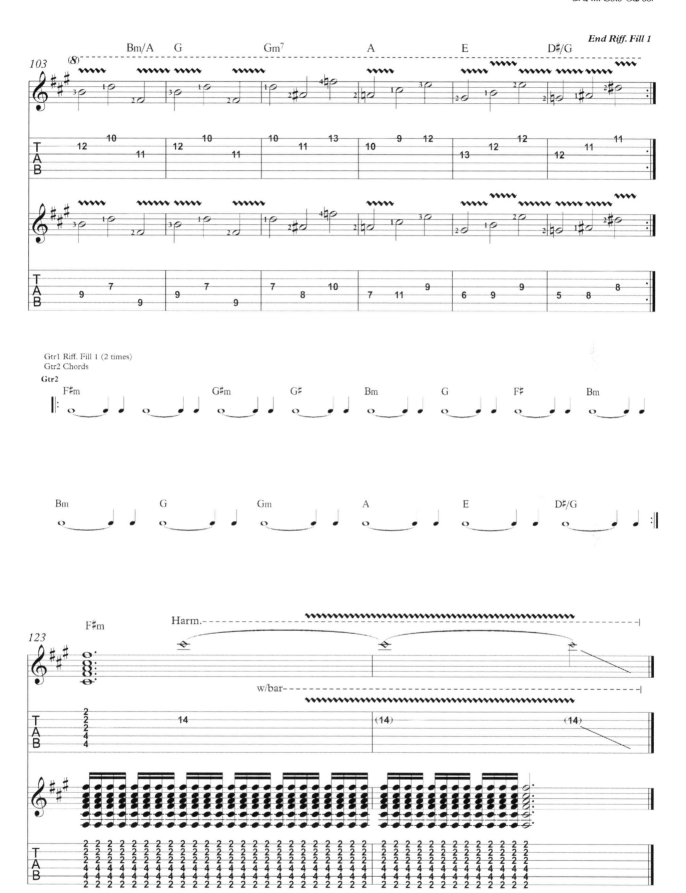

SHADOW OF THE HIEROPHANT
BY STEVE HACKETT, MIKE RUTHERFORD INTRO:

Intro:
|Ebm |B |Db |Ebm | |F |Bbm |C7(add4) |F | |F(add4) | | |

F   Am7/E
VEILING THE NIGHTSHADE

Dbmaj7/Ab   G   F   F9(sus4)
BRIDE STALKS A FLOWER REVEALED

F   Am7/E
NEARING THE HOUR MAKE

Dbmaj7/Ab   G   F   Gm11 |F/A F(add4)/Bb |Bb6/9 |
HASTE TO THEIR THRESHOLD CONCEALED

Dm7   C/E   Am   F/A Bb(add9)
LOST IN THOUGHT IN SEARCH OF VISION

Gm   Dm   Eb   Gm11 F Gm11 |F/A F(sus4)/Bb |Bb6/9 |
AS THE MOON ECLIPSED THE SUN

|Bb/Ab Ab6/9 Bb/Ab Ab6/9 Bb/Ab |Ab6/9 Bb/Ab Ab6/9 Bb/Ab

Intro

F   Am7/E
CASTING THE SAME STEPS

Dbmaj7/Ab   G   F   F9(sus4)
GLIMPSING HIS OWN FATE TO COME

F   Am7/E
MELT IN THE DREAM VOID

Dbmaj7/Ab   G   F   Gm11 |F/A F(add4)/Bb |Bb6/9 |
FROM WHICH HE NEVER CAN RUN

```
Dm7      C/E            Am       F/A    Bb(add9)
```
LOST IN THOUGHT IN SEARCH OF   VISION

```
Gm      Dm         Eb      Gm11   F     Gm11 |F/A  F(sus4)/Bb |Bb6/9          |
```
AS THE MOON ECLIPSED THE   SUN

```
|Bb/Ab  Ab6/9 Bb/Ab  Ab6/9 Bb/Ab  |Ab6/9 Bb/Ab  Ab6/9 Bb/Ab
```

Intro

```
F               Am7/E
```
TEARS FILL THE FOUNTAINS

```
Dbmaj7/Ab        G           F      F9(sus4)
```
BREAKING THEIR PROMISE TO HEAL

```
F               Am7/E
```
RIPPLING THE WATERS

```
Dbmaj7/Ab    G         F      Gm11   |F/A   F(add4)/Bb  |Bb6/9 |
```
MIRROR AN ENDED IDEAL

```
Dm7      C/E            Am       F/A   Bb(add9)
```
DEEP IN THOUGHT BUT ROBBED OF   VISION

```
Gm      Dm         Eb      Gm11   F     Gm11 |F/A  F(sus4)/Bb |Bb6/9          |
```
AS THE MOON ECLIPSED THE   SUN

```
|Bb/Ab  Ab6/9 Bb/Ab  Ab6/9 Bb/Ab  |Ab6/9 Bb/Ab  Ab6/9 Bb/Ab
```
Intro

Bridge Tapping

```
|G  |C  |F  |G  |G/B |A  |Bm  |A(sus4)/E  |        |D/F#   |E/G#

|D/F#   |E/G#   |A   |F#m A/E D |      |       |
```

Solo Theme

Play 6 times:
```
F#m |    |G#m  |G#  |Bm Bm/A  |G   |F#7/A#
|Bm |     Bm/A |G   |Gm7   |A  |E   |D#/G  |
```

F#m

WOLFLIGHT

Wolflight was recorded between 2014 and 2015. It was released in March 2015.With abundant sonorities, it was considered one of the best Progressive Rock albums of the year.

Studio Gears: Wolflight (2015)

LOVE SONG TO A VAMPIRE

Love Song to a Vampire has meticulous instrumentation. Steve played the introduction with the Oud and reverb. For the rest of the track he used a Yairi Nylon String and a Fernandes Goldtop 2002.

In the Yairi Classical Guitar Steve changed the tuning three times as following: low to high: E A D G B E; low to high: D G C F A D, and Gm6 tuning (low to high: D G D G Bb D).

1 - Fernandes Gold Top 2002
2 - Yairi Steel Black 1974
3 - Yairi Nylon Strings
4 - Banjo
5 - Oud
6 - Tiple
7 - Zemaitis 12 strings
8 - Line 6 DL4 Stompbox Modeler Delay
9 - Korg KVP-002 Volume Pedal
10 - SansAmp GT2 preamp Tech21
11 - DigiTech Whammy pedal
12 - Vox V847 Wah-Wah pedal (Fixed wah on full bass)
13 - AKG 414 (All acoustic guitars)
14 - Focusrite Red6 mic Pre amp (to record acoustic guitars with AKG)
15 - Urei 1175 Peak Limiter (to record acoustic guitars with AKG)
16 - Harmonica

Amanda Lehmann sang with Steve on this track and she added the vocal part to the choruses to give breadth to the harmonies. In the last chorus, she chose a melody that counterpointed the main vocal, which brought an extra dimension to that sequence. For the shows, keyboard player Roger King created a choir-like vocal sound copying these lines in the last chorus.

from Steve Hackett - *Wolflight*

Love Song To a Vampire

by Steve Hackett

Transcribed by Paulo De Carvalho

*Gtr. 1 Oud (Lute) arr. for Gtr.

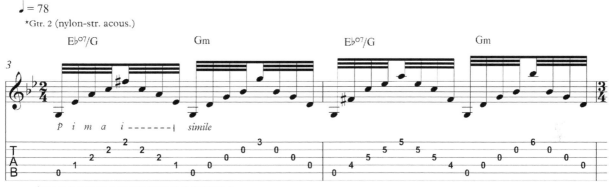

*Gtr. 2: Gm6 tuning (low to high) D-G-D-G-Bb-E

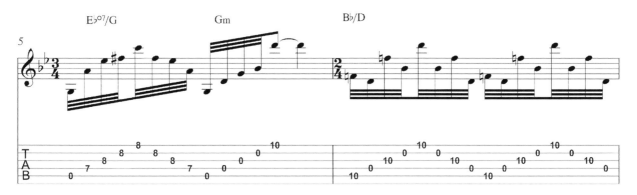

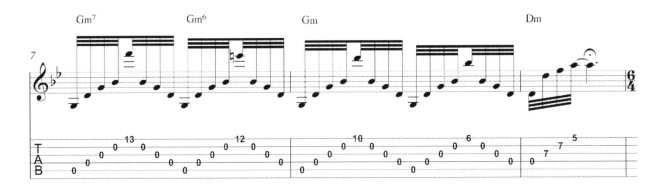

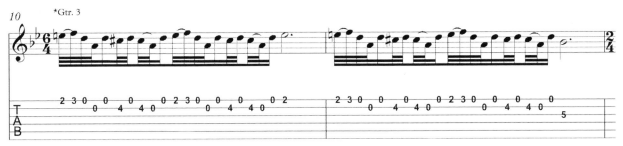

*Gtr. 3: Tuning (low to high) D-G-C-F-A-D

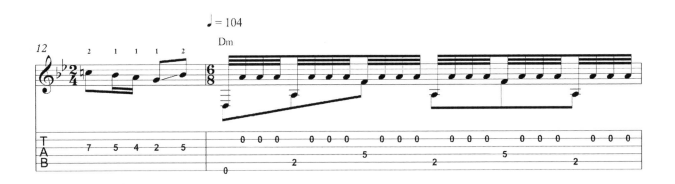

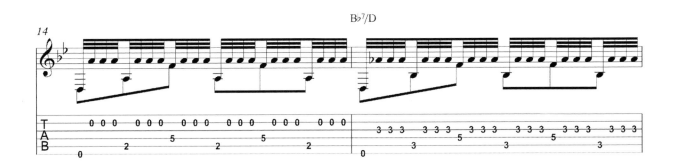

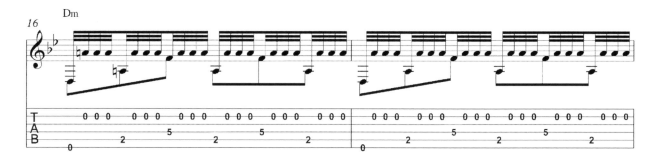

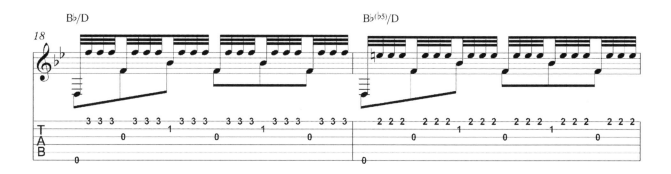

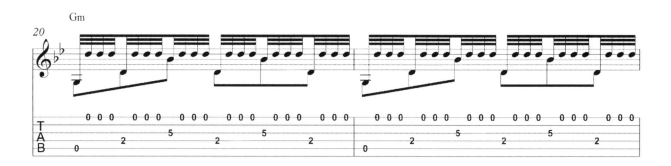

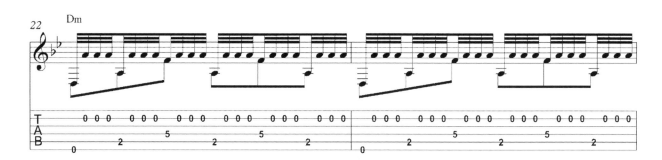

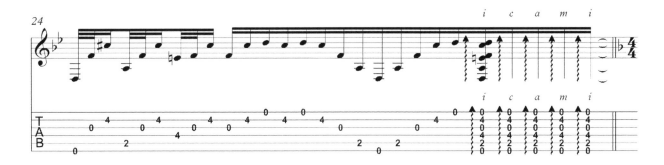

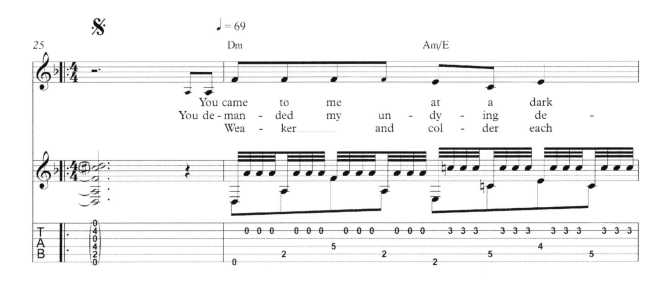

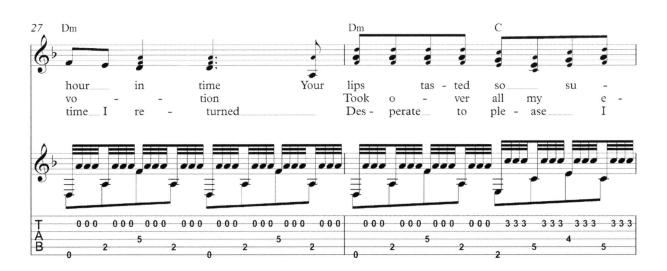

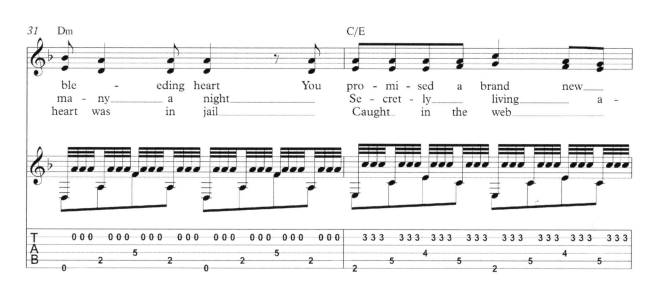

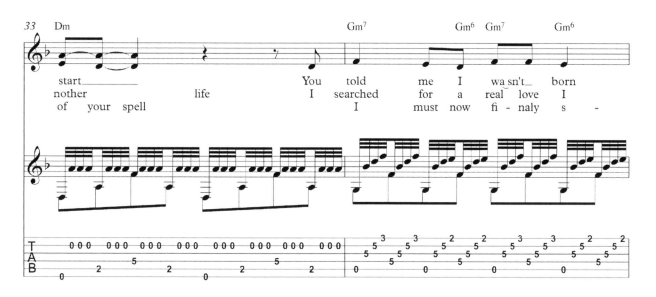

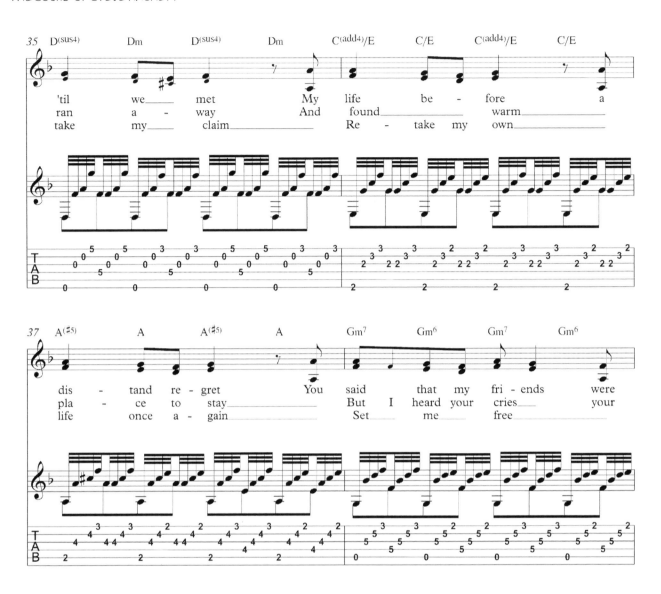

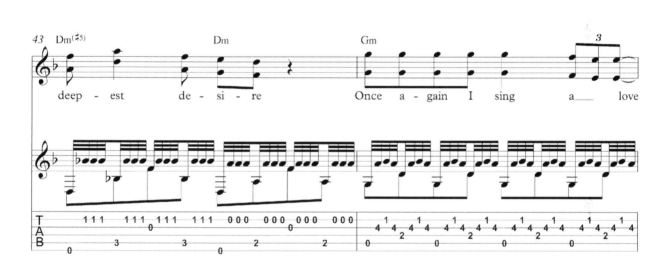

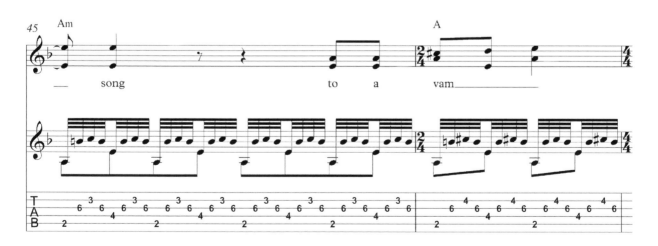

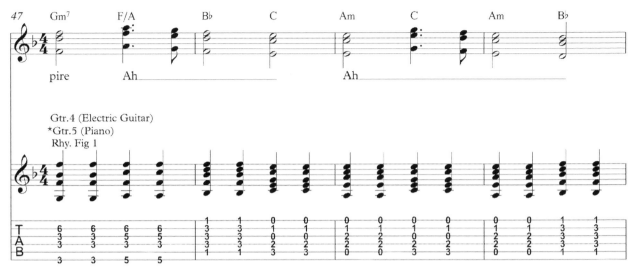

*Gtr. 5 - Piano arr. for gtr

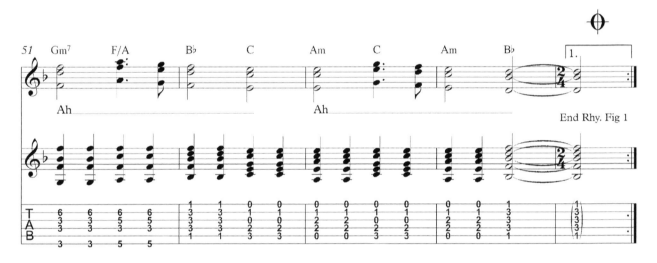

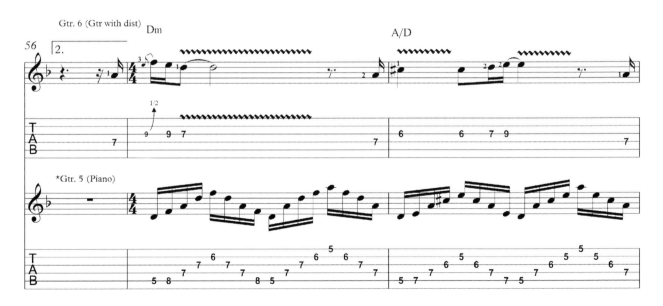

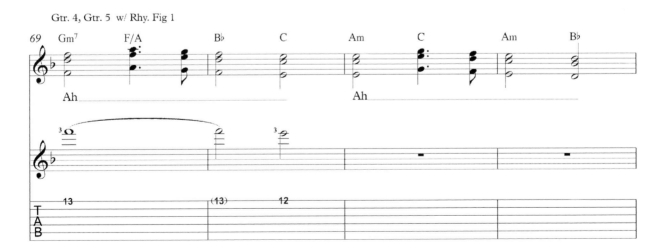

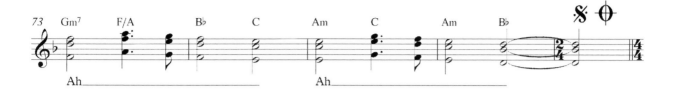

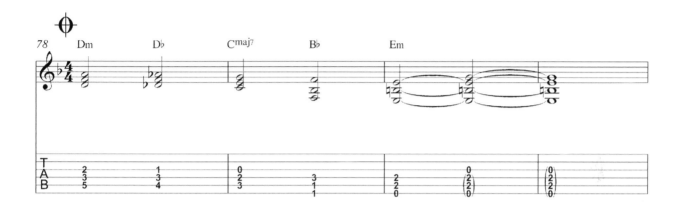

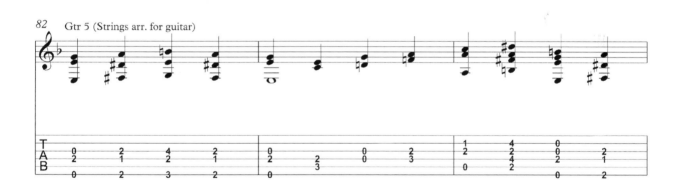

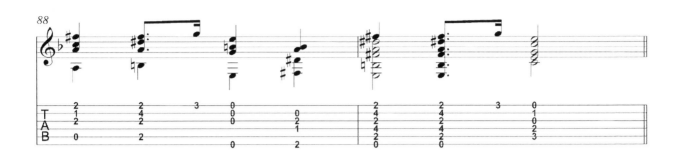

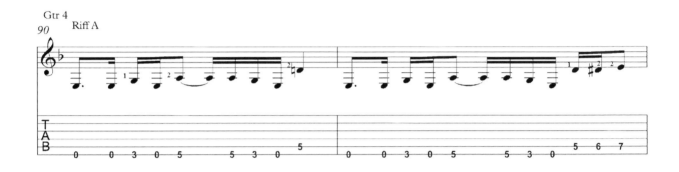

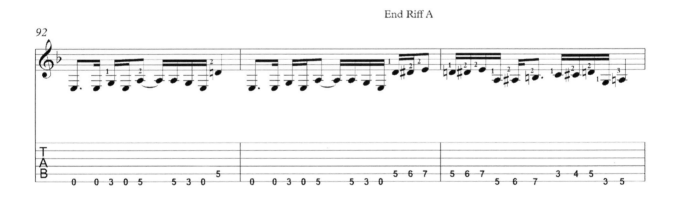

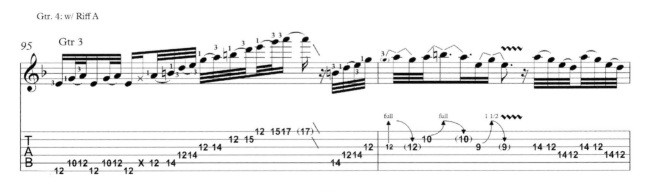

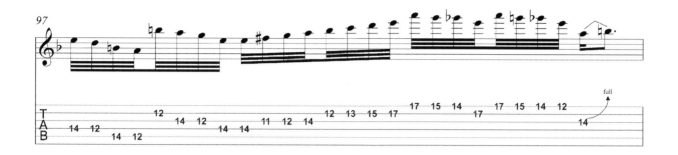

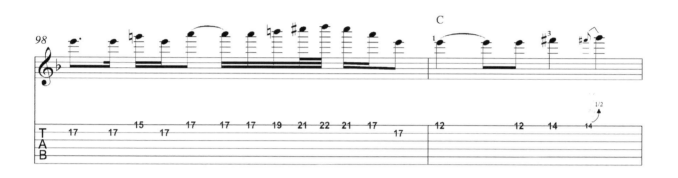

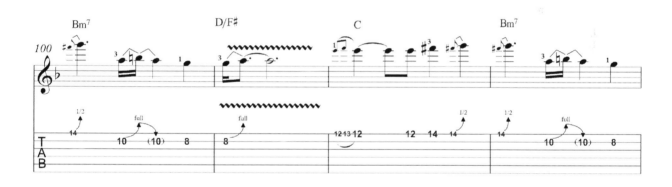

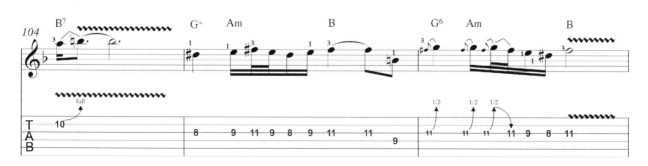

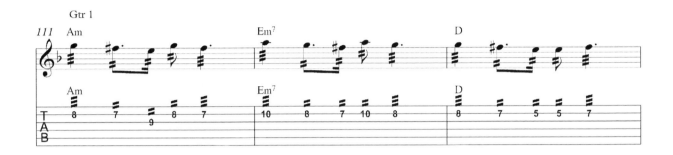

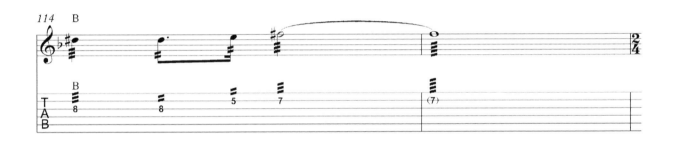

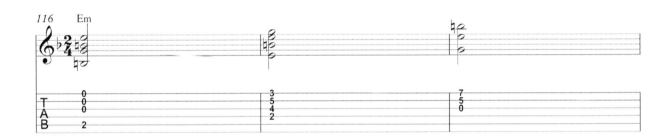

Photos 33 – 37: Steve Hackett in concert. Fort Lauderdale, US, April 14th , 2016

LOVE SONG TO A VAMPIRE
BY STEVE HACKETT

Intro:

```
|        |Ebdim/G Gm  |Ebdim/G Gm  |Ebdim/G Gm  |Bb/D     |
|Gm7 Gm6 |Gm  |Dm  |    |    |    |    |    |    |
|Bb7/D   |Dm  |    |Bb  |Bb(b5)/D  |B  |Gm  |    |
|Dm  |    |    |    |    |
```

    Dm   **Am/E**   **Dm**
YOU CAME TO ME AT A DARK HOUR IN TIME

       Dm   **C/E**   **Dm**
YOUR LIPS TASTED SO SUBLIME

    C/E   **Dm**
YOU DRANK IN MY HOPES, MY BLEEDING HEART

    C/E   **Dm**
YOU PROMISED ME A BRAND NEW START

   Gm7   **Gm6** **Gm7**   **Gm6** **D(sus4)** **Dm** **D(sus4)** **Dm**
YOU TOLD ME I WASN'T BORN 'TIL WE MET

    C(add4)/E **C/E** **C(add4)/E** **C/E** **A(#5)** **A** **A(#5)** **A**
MY LIFE   BEFORE   A DISTANT REGRET

    Gm7 Gm6   **Gm7**   **Gm6**   **D(sus4)** **Dm**   **D(sus4)** **Dm**
YOU SAID THAT MY FRIENDS WERE NO GOOD FOR ME

    C(add4)/E **C/E** **C(add4)/E** **C/E**   **A(#5)** **A** **A(#5)** **A**
YOU CLAIMED ONLY YOU COULD SET ME FREE

   Dm7   **Dm6**   **Dm(#5)**   **Dm**
EACH TIME YOU ENSLAVE ME TO YOUR DEEPEST DESIRE

Gm   **Am**   **A** **Gm7**
ONCE AGAIN I SING A LOVE SONG TO A VAMPIRE

 Gm7   **F/A** |**Bb** **C** |**Am** **C** |**Am** **Bb** |(repeat) (Bridge)
AH

    Dm   **Am/E**   **Dm**
YOU DEMANDED MY UNDYING DEVOTION

 Dm   **C/E**   **Dm**
TOOK OVER ALL MY EMOTIONS

C/E   **Dm**
BUT YOU WERE AWAY FOR MANY A NIGHT

C/E   **Dm**
SECRETLY LIVING ANOTHER LIFE

 Gm7   **Gm6**   **Gm7** **Gm6** **D(sus4)** **Dm** **Dm(sus4)** **Dm**
I SEARCHED FOR A REAL LOVE, I RAN AWAY

   C(add4)/E **C/E** **C(add4)/E** **C/E** **A(#5)** **A**   **A(#5)** **A**
AND FOUND A WARM PLACE TO STAY

Gm7 Gm6   **Gm7 Gm6**   **D(sus4)** **Dm**   **D(sus4)** **Dm**
BUT I HEARD YOUR CRIES, YOUR ANGER, YOUR LIES

C(add4)/E C/E   C(add4)/E C/E A(#5)   A   A(#5) A
A FLASH   OF YOUR EYES   PULLED ME BACK INSIDE
         Dm7   Dm6
EACH TIME YOU ENSLAVE ME
         Dm(#5)   Dm
TO YOUR DEEPEST DESIRE
Gm   **Am**   **A   Gm7**
ONCE AGAIN I SING A LOVE SONG TO A VAMPIRE

 Gm7   F/A |Bb   C |Am   C |Am   Bb | (repeat)
AH

SOLO
|Dm |A/D |A A7 |A(b9)/C# Dm7 |D7 Gm7 |C F/A |Gm7 Gm7/A |
|A A(b9) |Dm7 Dm7(b6) |Dm6 Dm7 |Gm7 |A A(#5) A |

Gm7   F/A |Bb   C |Am   C |Am   Bb | (repeat)
AH

Dm   **Am/E**   **Dm**
WEAKER AND COLDER EACH TIME I RETURNED
Dm   **C/E**   **Dm**
DESPERATE TO PLEASE I NEVER LEARNED
     C/E   **Dm**
THE DOOR WAS UNLOCKED BUT MY HEART WAS IN JAIL
C/E   **Dm**
CAUGHT IN THE WEB OF YOUR SPELL
Gm7   Gm6 Gm7   Gm6 D(sus4) Dm   D(sus4) Dm
I MUST NOW FINALLY   STAKE   MY CLAIM
C(add4)/E C/E   C(add4)/E C/E A(#5) A   A(#5)   A
RE   - TAKE MY OWN   LIFE ONCE AGAIN
Gm7   Gm6 Gm7 Gm6 D(sus4)   Dm D(sus4)   Dm
SET   ME   FREE,   LET   ME BREATHE
C(add4)/E C/E   C(add4)/E C/E A(#5)   A   A(#5)   A
I'LL   SHED THE SUNLIGHT   ON   YOUR DECEIT
         Dm7   Dm6
EACH TIME YOU ENSLAVE ME
         Dm(#5)   Dm
TO YOUR DEEPEST DESIRE
Gm   **Am**   **A   Gm7**
ONCE AGAIN I SING A LOVE SONG TO A VAMPIRE
Bridge 2 to Riff and solo to end

135

LIVE AT THE NEW THEATRE (PREMONITIONS)

Live at The New Theatre, Oxford, July 1ˢᵗ, 1979, was first released in 2015 within the box set collection *Premonitions* of early recordings 1975-1983. It featured ten CDs, which included Steve's first four albums in stereo plus four live shows never before released (including *Live at The New Theatre*), and four DVDs with the same first four albums, but in 5.1.

NARNIA

Narnia was inspired by the book *The Lion, The Witch and The Wardrobe* by C.S. Lewis.

The song was originally part of Steve's second solo album *Please Don't Touch* with Steve Walsh from Kansas in the vocals. Steve used: two acoustics guitars in stereo, Fender Stratocaster in the middle, and an Eventide Harmonizer on all three guitars for the introduction; Jazz Chorus amp and Les Paul with slide and Bow for the rest.

In *Live at The New Theatre 1979* Steve played a Fender Stratocaster with his brother, John Hackett, playing a Giffin guitar with a Boss Chorus pedal.

In the first part of this recording, Pete Hicks sang " It's just happens *boys and girls* who shout come out to play", in contrast with Steve Walsh, who sang " It's just happens *girls and boys* who shout come out to play" in the studio album.

Live Gears : Live at The New Theatre, Oxford (1st July 1979)

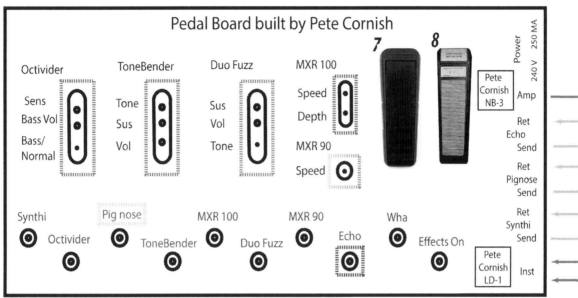

Pedal Board built by Pete Cornish

1 - Gibson Les Paul Gold Top 1957
2 - Fender Stratocaster (Normal tuning)
3 - Roland GR-500 Guitar Synthesizer
4 - Fender Stratocaster(Tuning in E Major)
5 - Yari Classic Alvarez Guitar
6 - Ebow
7 - Cry Baby Wah-Wah
8 - Schaller Volume Pedal F121
9 - Colorsound Octivider
10 - Colorsound Supa Tone Bender
11 - Shaftesbury Duo Fuzz
12 - MXR Phase 90
13 - MXR Phase 100
14 - Pignose(He used to put his harmonica)
15 - Echoplex EP-3 Tape Echo
16 - EMS Synth Hi-fli
17 - Marshall 100w (Clean)
18 - Marshall 1987x50w (Full cracked distortion)
19 - Ernie Ball light 12 strings
20 - Fender 6 strings 0.10"
21 - Plastic pick-Fender medium

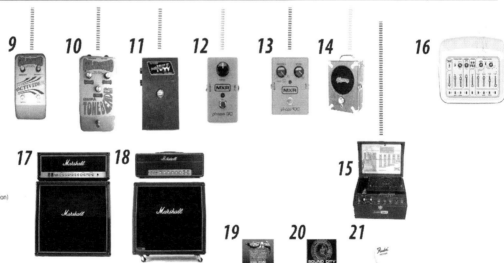

Signal Routing:

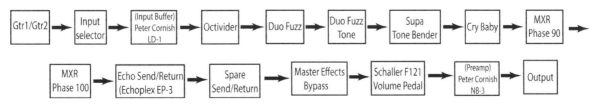

Gtr1/Gtr2 → Input selector → (Input Buffer) Peter Cornish LD-1 → Octivider → Duo Fuzz → Duo Fuzz Tone → Supa Tone Bender → Cry Baby → MXR Phase 90

MXR Phase 100 → Echo Send/Return (Echoplex EP-3 → Spare Send/Return → Master Effects Bypass → Schaller F121 Volume Pedal → (Preamp) Peter Cornish NB-3 → Output

from Steve Hackett - *Premonitions - Live in Oxford New Theatre*

Narnia

by Steve Hackett

Transcribed by Paulo De Carvalho

Gtr. 1: (low to high) E-B-E-G#-B-E

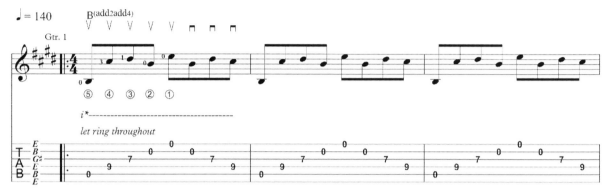

i* - Steve use the index finger like a pick

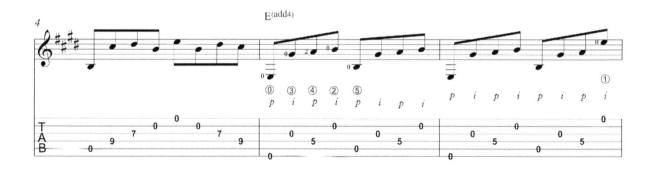

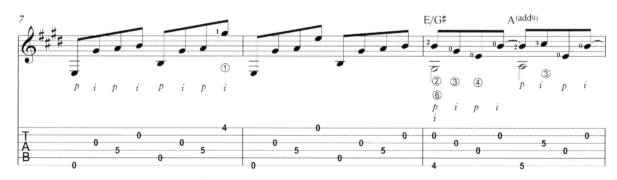

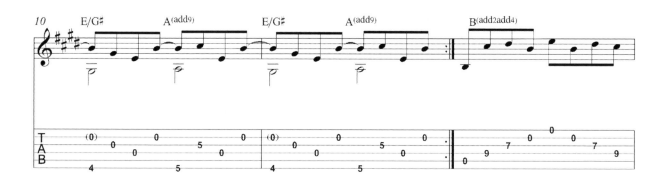

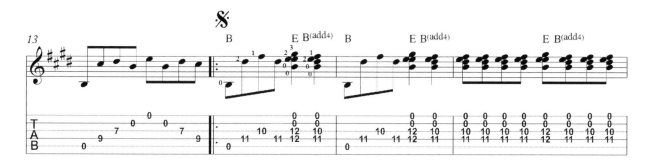

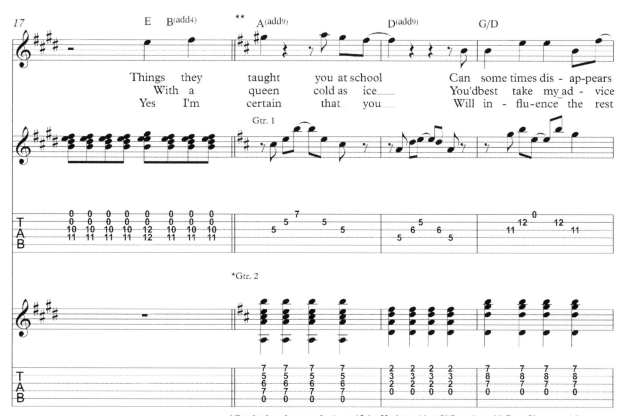

Things they taught you at school Can some times dis - ap-pears
With a queen cold as ice You'dbest take my ad - vice
Yes I'm certain that you Will in - flu-ence the rest

Gtr. 1

*Gtr. 2

*Gtr. 2 tcl. and gtr arr. for 1 gtr. (John Hackett with a Giffin guitar with Boss Chorus pedal)
★★ *Chords symbols reflect implied harmony*

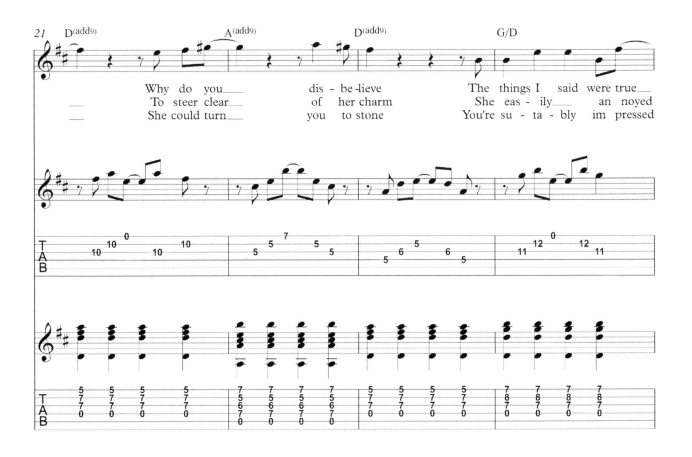

Why do you____ dis - be -lieve The things I said were true____
To steer clear____ of her charm She eas - ily____ an noyed
She could turn____ you to stone You're su - ta - bly im pressed

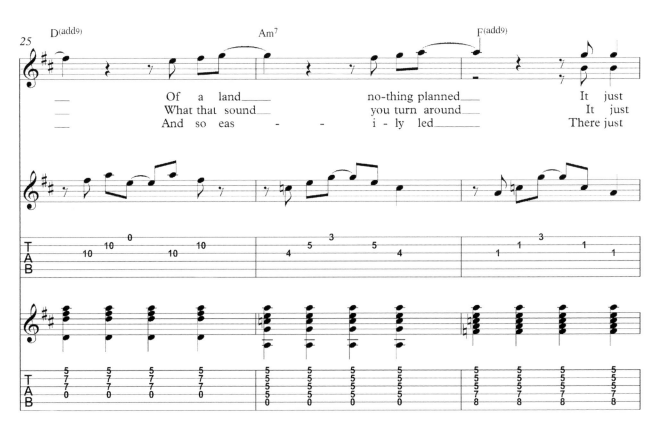

Of a land____ no-thing planned____ It just
What that sound____ you turn around____ It just
And so eas - - i - ly led____ There just

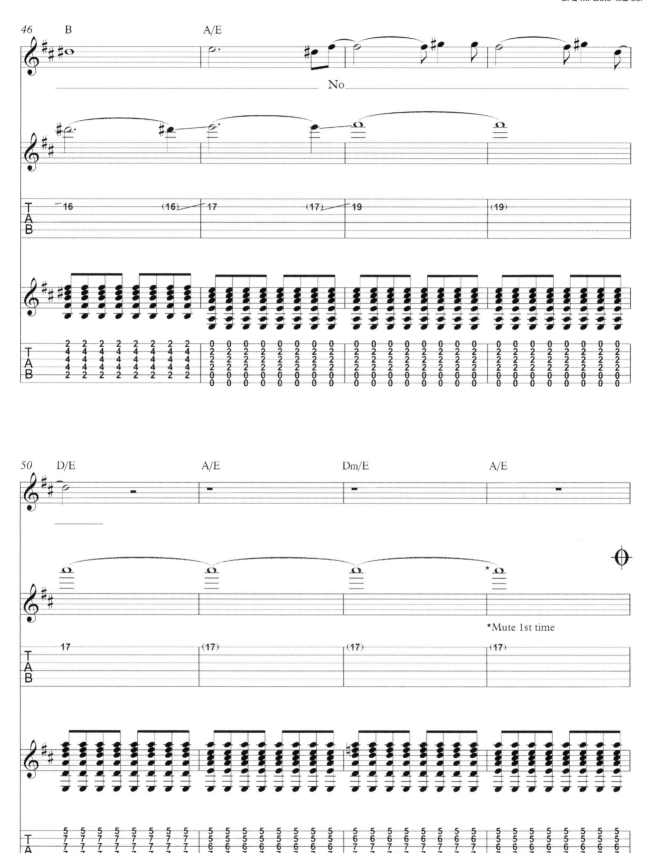

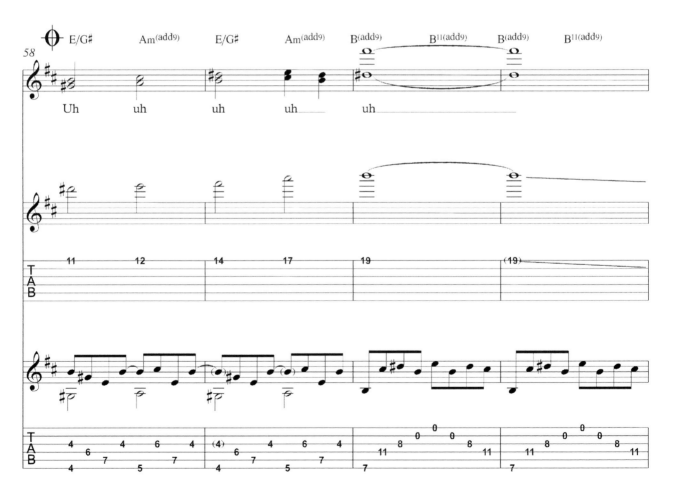

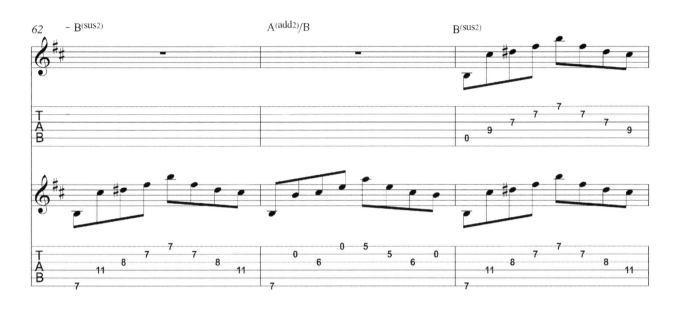

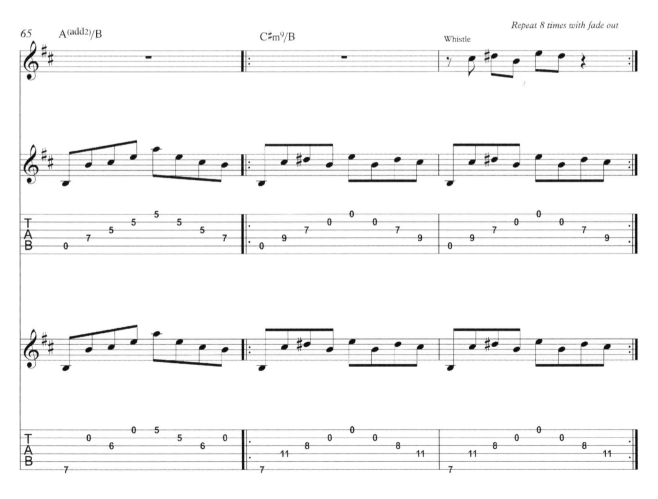

NARNIA
BY STEVE HACKETT

Intro:
|B(add2add4) | | | |E(add4) | | | |E/G#   A(add9) |
E/G#   A(add9) |E/G#   A9(add9) | |B(add2add4) |

       A(add9)   D(add9)
THINGS THEY TAUGHT YOU AT SCHOOL
      G/D   D(add9)
CAN SOMETIMES DISAPPEAR
        A(add9)   D(add9)
WHY DO YOU DISBELIEVE
      G/D   D(add9)
THE THINGS I SAID WERE TRUE
    Am7   F(add9)
OF A LAND NOTHING PLANNED
      G/D   C/D
IT JUST HAPPENS BOYS AND GIRLS WHO
Dm7   A(add4) A B(Add2add4)
SHOUT COME OUT   TO PLAY

| B(add2add4) | Repeat 5X

     A(add9)   D(add9)
WITH A QUEEN COLD AS ICE
      G/D   D(add9)
YOU'D BEST TAKE MY ADVICE
       A(add9)   D(add9)
TO STEER CLEAR OF HER CHARMS
      G/D   D(add9)
SHE'S EASILY ANNOYED
        Am7   F(add9)
WHAT'S THAT SOUND, YOU TURN AROUND
        G/D   C/D
THERE JUST HAPPEN THERE ARE BELLS
    Dm7   A(add4) A   B(add2add4)
AND REINDEERS DRAWING A SLEIGH
   B   A/E
OH THERE TROUBLED WITH SNOW   COVERED PEAKS

```
         B                          A/E
TILL THE END     OF TIME
B    A/E
OH
B                              A/E
 WE KNOW YOU'RE A DAUGHTER OF EVE
         B              A/E
AND A FRIEND OF MINE


|B   |A/E  |B    |A/E  |    |    |
|D   |A/E  |Dm/E |A/E  |       |B(add2add4)  |


        A(add9)          D(add9)
YES I'M CERTAIN THAT YOU
         G/D
WILL INFLUENCE THE REST
            A(add9)          D(add9)
SHE COULD TURN YOU TO STONE
        G/D                 D(add9)
YOU'RE SUITABLY IMPRESSED
        Am7        F(add9)
AND SO EASILY LED
              G/D     C/D        Dm7
THERE JUST HAPPEN TO BE REPERCUSSIONS
A(add4)  A   B
MONTHS AHEAD


    B                            A/E
OH THERE TROUBLED WITH SNOW    COVERED PEAKS


        B                         A/E
TILL THE END     OF TIME
B    A/E
OH
B                              A/E
 WE KNOW YOU'RE A DAUGHTER OF EVE
         B              A/E
AND A FRIEND OF MINE


|E/G#  Am(add9) |E/G#  Am(add9) |B(add9)   B11(add9) |B(add9)   B11(add9) |
|B(sus2)   |A(add2)/B   |B(sus2)   |A(add2)/B
||C#m9/B   |       || Fade
```

THE SOUND OF STEVE HACKETT

THE TOTAL EXPERIENCE
LIVE IN LIVERPOOL

This is a live performance on the British leg of the 2015 tour. In the concert, one of the gears that Steve had in the pedalboard was a Behringer FC 1010, which controlled the rack by Midi. On the rack there were two zoom 9030 (one being used and one spare), which are the last in line after the pedal board. Steve used mono in and stereo out to the Marshall heads.

LOVING SEA

Composed in a boat on a trip to Mexico, and having been inspired by a stunning day, *Loving Sea* has music and lyrics by Steve and Jo Hackett. In this live version, Steve and Roine Stolt were on the vocals and the guitars (Steve played on the Zemaitis 12 strings); Gary O'Toole on the percussion and vocals; Rob Townsend on the flute, Amanda Lehmann on the vocal, and Roger King on the keyboard.

Amanda testified that *Loving Sea* is a gentle, cheerful tune that made her smile when she sang it. She did not sing this track on the album *Wolflight*, but after its release, Steve and she decided to do a vocal duet of it for a radio show. It was so well received, that they kept doing it in their live shows. *Live in Liverpool DVD* included the duet, being a differentiating mark to *Wolflight*.

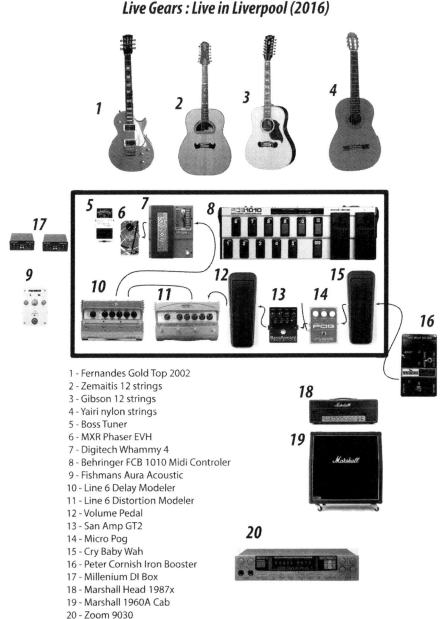

Live Gears : Live in Liverpool (2016)

1 - Fernandes Gold Top 2002
2 - Zemaitis 12 strings
3 - Gibson 12 strings
4 - Yairi nylon strings
5 - Boss Tuner
6 - MXR Phaser EVH
7 - Digitech Whammy 4
8 - Behringer FCB 1010 Midi Controler
9 - Fishmans Aura Acoustic
10 - Line 6 Delay Modeler
11 - Line 6 Distortion Modeler
12 - Volume Pedal
13 - San Amp GT2
14 - Micro Pog
15 - Cry Baby Wah
16 - Peter Cornish Iron Booster
17 - Millenium DI Box
18 - Marshall Head 1987x
19 - Marshall 1960A Cab
20 - Zoom 9030

Amanda chose a country style of vocal for the verses, and a lighter, flowing style for the choruses, in where she gradually faded the vocals in to match the floating quality of the section. The song reminds Amanda of a glistening sea. For her, music is very visual.

from Steve Hackett - *Live in Liverpool*

Loving Sea

by Steve Hackett, Jo Hackett

Transcribed by Paulo De Carvalho

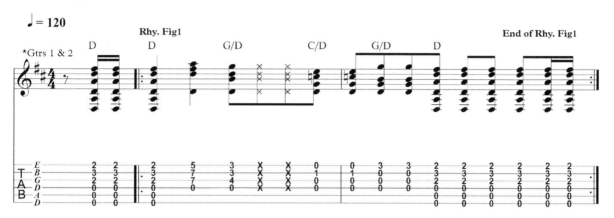

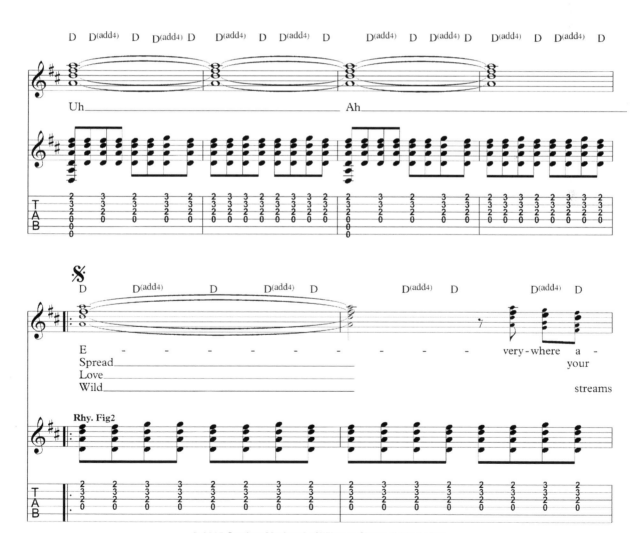

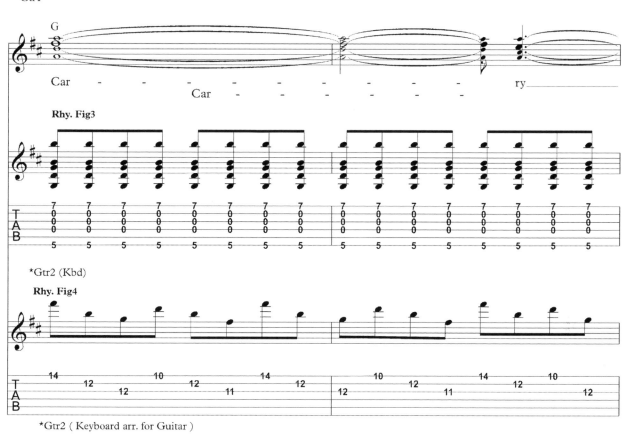

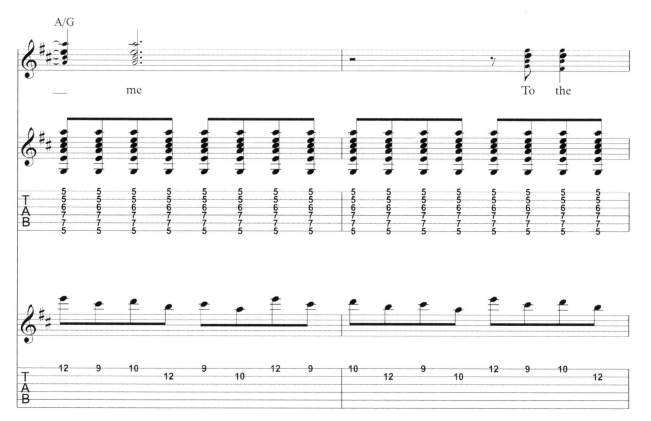

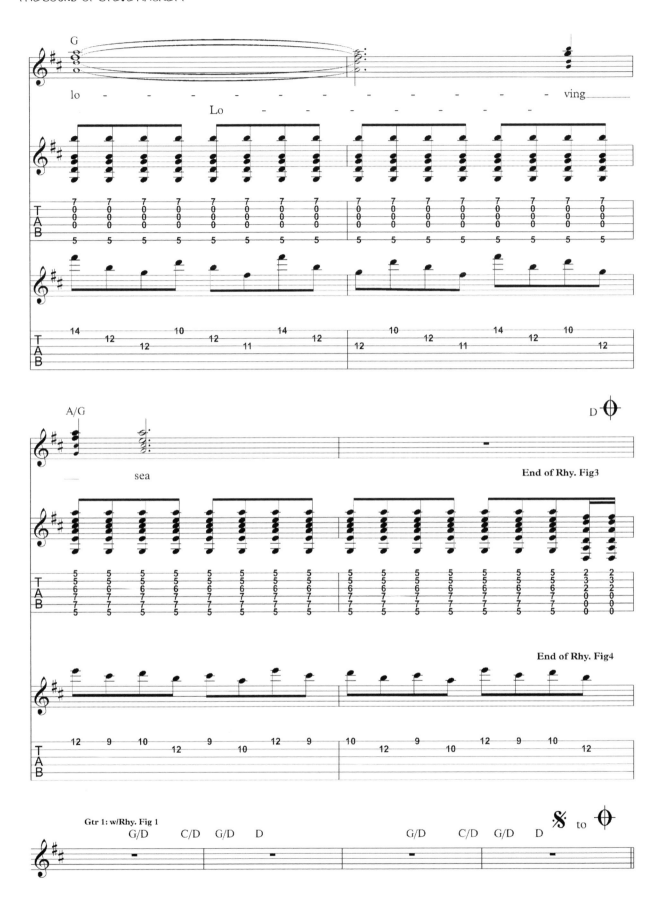

High, High a - bove the wor - ld _____ (High a - bout the

world) Deep in the co - lour of your lo - ve _____

Gtr 1: w/Rhy. Fig 1

Solo Flute

Gtr 1: w/Rhy. Fig 2

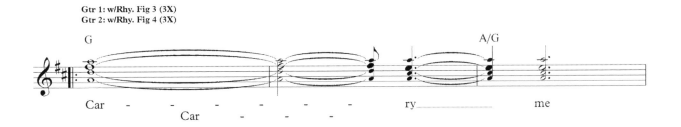

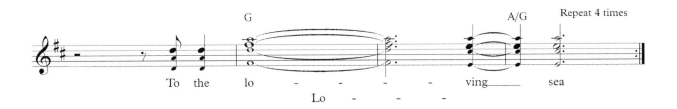

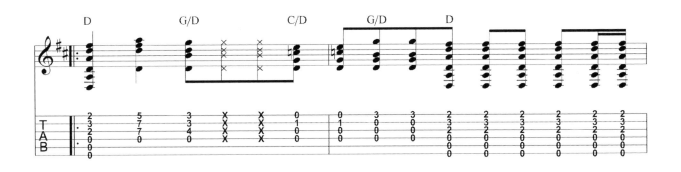

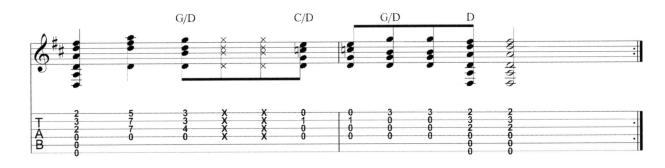

LOVING SEA
BY STEVE HACKETT, JO HACKETT

Intro: D D G/D C/D G/D D
        D D G/D C/D G/D D (D   D4 D D4 D D4 D)

(D   D4 D D4 D D4 D)
Oh........Ah.........

D   **C**
EVERYWHERE AROUND YOU BLUE, BLUE SEA
Bm7   **A7**
ANY BOAT AT ALL AS LONG AS IT'S YOU AND ME

D   **C**
SPREAD YOUR WINGS WON'T YOU BE MY GUIDE
Bm7   **A7**
ALL ALONG THE WAY ON LIFE'S LONG, LONG RICH RIDE

G   A/G   **G A/G**
CARRY   ME TO THE LOVING   SEA

D D G/D C/D G/D D D D G/D C/D G/D D

D   **C**
LOVE TUMBLING FROM STONES AND WATERFALLS
Bm7   **A7**
ON TO THE PAGES DREAMS TAKE SHAPE TO YOUR WAKE UP   CALL

D   **C**
WILD STREAMS WON'T YOU BE MY GUIDE
Bm7   **A7**
ALL ALONG THE WAY ON LIFE'S LONG, LONG RICH   RIDE

G   A/G   **G A/G**
CARRY   ME TO THE LOVING   SEA

D   **G/D**
HIGH, HIGH ABOVE THE WORLD
D   **G/D**
DEEP IN THE COLOUR OF YOUR LOVE

D D G/D C/D G/D D D D G/D C/D G/D D
D   C   Bm7   A7

G   A/G   **G A/G**
CARRY   ME TO THE LOVING SEA (4 TIMES)

155

PHOTO GALLERY

Paulo De Carvalho(left) and Steve Hackett (right)

Paulo De Carvalho(left) and Pete Cornish (right)

Paulo De Carvalho (left) and Steve Hackett (right)

Jo Hackett, Steve Hackett and Paulo De Carvalho

*From left to right: Paulo De Carvalho, Jo Hackett,
Steve Hackett and Ivo De Carvalho*

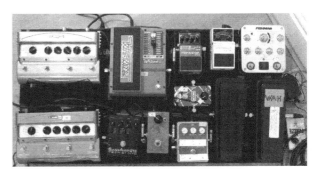

*Steve's pedalboard used in the album
The Night Siren (released on March 24th, 2017)*

ABOUT THE AUTHOR

PAULO DE CARVALHO is a guitarist, composer, arranger and audio engineer.

He earned a bachelor in musical composition through the Federal University of Rio de Janeiro, Brazil.

He was granted the *Cultural Merit Award* from *Acontece Magazine* (2008, 2009, 2010) and he was nominated for the *Brazilian Press Award* as best Brazilian musician in the US (2008, 2009, 2010, 2011, 2012, 2013).

He performs and tours regularly playing Brazilian Jazz.

www.paulodecarvalhogtr.com

Printed in Great Britain
by Amazon